feast

OF LIFE

feast
OF LIFE

SPIRITUAL FOOD FOR BALANCED LIVING

JO KADLECEK

FOREWORD BY KELLY K. MONROE

Baker Books

A Division of Baker Book House Co
Grand Rapids, Michigan 49516

Published by Baker Books
a division of Baker Book House Company
P.O. Box 6287, Grand Rapids, MI 49516-6287

Printed in the United States of America

Library of Congress Cataloging-in-Publication Data

Kadlecek, Jo.
    Feast of life : spiritual food for balanced living /
Jo Kadlecek : foreword by Kelly K. Monroe.
      p.   cm.
    Includes bibliographical references.
    ISBN 0-8010-5947-X (pbk.)
    1. Christian life. I. Title.
BV4501.2.K23 1999
248.4—dc21   99-22038

Scripture quotations are from the HOLY BIBLE, NEW INTERNATIONAL VERSION®. NIV®. Copyright © 1973, 1978, 1984 by International Bible Society. Used by permission of Zondervan Publishing House. All rights reserved.

For current information about all releases from Baker Book House, visit our web site:

                http://www.bakerbooks.com

To
my sister, Andrea,
whose perpetual quest to live
a radically balanced life with Christ
inspires me and many others to do the same

The one who feeds on me will live because of me.
JOHN 6:57

CONTENTS

Foreword   9
Preface   11
Acknowledgments   13

1 "Pass Me the Balance"   15
2 Solitude: Breakfast with Jesus   33
3 Solitude: Setting the Table for One   49
4 Service: Chopping Those Onions   65
5 Service: Working in the Kitchen   85
6 Community: Sharing the Meal   107
7 Community: Eating Together   125
8 Contemplation: Savoring Each Morsel   145
9 Contemplation: Taste, Smell, Enjoy   165
10 The Dessert Tray   185

Notes   197
Bibliography   201

FOREWORD

A month or so ago, Jo Kadlecek and her kindly husband, Chris, slipped out of New York City. I retreated from Cambridge. We planned to meet up for dinner. That's all.

We got beyond the centripetal force of our cities, crowded with ambition, complexity, haste, pride, hunger, and activity, which at least suggests life filled with meaning.

We met on a humble farm, with sappy pine trees and bouncing (slobbering) golden retrievers, wind and music, and the kind of quiet that thaws one's soul.

Somehow that meal became a moment. It became an evening, and then a morning: an unrushed time out of time together in a cabin surrounded by melting snow and the first signs of spring.

This was a meal that lasted for hours, with time enough to taste and to feel and to savor God's creation. There was time enough to listen and to hear one another. Time enough to exhale the pollution and let the world's anesthetic wear off. Time enough to breathe in the spirit of holiness and wholeness. Time to begin to be re-covered by God in the shelter of one another.

We took turns behind the piano and guitar. We remembered childhood stories, the adventures of growing up on skis, and biking through Ireland together. We spoke of our work with racial reconciliation (Jo and Chris), and silly recreation (Kelly). We spoke of the loveliness of a communal and symphonic Christian presence in a disintegrating world—that is, the love of God as the light of the world, more hopeful than the easy curse of darkness. We spoke of Jesus, the person of truth and grace, as the light for Harlem, for Harvard, for the whole cosmos with or without our knowing.

Reclining before the fire, we even had time for that which is rarely spoken: candid reflections on exhaustion, battles, heartbreaks, and good grief that keeps us pressing on because of the character of God, whatever befalls.

God gave us yet another day, and in that morning someone put the tea kettle on the stove. The neighbors dropped off raspberry jam, and the chickens gave us their eggs. We held one another's hands as we paused for grace.

We must keep pausing for grace. This book is a pause for grace, and it (like its author) is full of grace.

What I see, now that I have read this beautiful book, is that our time together was more than a few meals: It was a feast of life. It was a moment saturated by the memory and presence of the one who is our Feast, our daily bread and living water, the lover of our souls and the life of the party who converted the grapes of wrath into the new wine of joy.

He, and Jo Kadlecek, invite us to a feast. They have the boldness to suggest that if we will drink from one particular wellspring and eat of food that we may not yet know, then we will never thirst or hunger again. They are offering us food that makes the whole of life a feast.

If this spiritual food sustains Jo Kadlecek in Harlem, in inner cities where she is working with the poor and forgotten, in the hard work of racial reconciliation among the least, the last, and the lost, then it is bread for the world indeed. It is food for the hunger of the new millennium and the fuel for the challenges we will face. She has my attention, and respect, and affection.

Here, in these pages, we can learn the recipe for this abundant feast of love and life. And may our taste buds awaken for the journey.

KELLY K. MONROE

PREFACE

Some of my greatest moments in life have taken place around a table of food. If you've ever had the privilege of sitting down with people you love to participate in a meal you spent days preparing, you know there is very little that compares. Between bites of bread and sips of wine, you chat about who's going where, what's happening when, how everyone's feeling. It is so much more than eating a meal; it is emotional and bonding, rich and fulfilling. Sacred even.

Life is a feast. Or at least it's supposed to be. The Bible often uses the metaphor of the banquet table to describe the great life—heaven—one full of delicious celebration and satisfying morsels of fellowship. It is where we taste and smell and indulge in the goodness of God, delighting in the fact that we can never get enough. It is *the* meal of all meals, one that costs all we have and is worth more than we could ever spend. And though it is gloriously worth looking forward to, I believe portions of heaven are available to us for delightful nourishment in the here and now. In fact, we can enjoy an unmovable feast every day.

When American writer Ernest Hemingway first penned his book *A Moveable Feast*, he was writing of his young days in Paris just after World War I. He talked of all that fed his creative hunger—the rich and satisfying days in the exuberant French city and the literary camaraderie he enjoyed there. Though he was able to carry pieces of that "feast" with him throughout his sad but enormous writing life, harsh reality tells us that Hemingway's feast eventually ended. No human efforts, however exquisite, can last forever.

However, in John 21 when we watch Jesus *after* his death on the cross inviting the disciples to join him for breakfast, we know that his is an unmovable feast. He calls us to an eternal banquet that begins today. He invites us to eat well, to savor each morsel, to enjoy flavors and aromas and textures. And he does so by commanding us to eat together, to be willing to chop the onions and set the table in preparation for a nourishing and joyful time with him and with others.

It is a balanced meal that Jesus serves us, a feast that, in turn, gives us balance to serve others. It is the unending, sustaining, healthy Christian life, one so tasty that others ask to be invited.

As the psalmist describes it: "You prepare a table before me in the presence of my enemies. You anoint my head with oil; my cup overflows. Surely goodness and love will follow me all the days of my life, and I will dwell in the house of the LORD forever" (Ps. 23:5–6).

Bon appétit!

ACKNOWLEDGMENTS

Just like every good community dinner is the result of many hands and creative recipes, so, too, is a book project the result of many kind and helpful friends. To these, I wish to offer a table full of thanks: Kathy, Tyler, Daniel, Patty, Bob, Nancy, Jamie, Lanita, Terrence, Andi, Andy, Joel, and the other friends in the college and career Sunday school class at Church in the City in Denver, Colorado, who initially asked the question, "So how do we stay balanced and keep the faith for the long haul?" which started it all; the incredibly gifted writer Bernie Sheahan, who (in Oxford, Mississippi) first suggested this material might actually be a book and then made me believe it could be; Sara Fortenberry, my literary agent, who reinforced Bernie's confidence and persevered with the proposal until we found the right publisher; the Racial Unity Ministry home fellowship group at Redeemer Presbyterian Church in New York City, who allowed me to "experiment" this material on them; Joseph and Connie Ricci and their sister, Honja Metroka, whose consistent enthusiasm for these principles has encouraged me greatly; Scotty Smith and Ellen Walsh, whose gifts of hospitality allowed me to write in their respective homes and provided a blessed refuge; my New York community of friends, Laura, Kristy, Melissa, Dan, Andrea, Butch, and Elvon, whose patience with me during the writing process was nothing short of miraculous; Bob Hosack at Baker (and the rest of the Baker staff), whose professionalism, vision, and confidence have made this experience a publishing pleasure; the brilliant, unassuming, and wonderfully Irish Kelly Monroe, whose bicycling friendship and willingness to write the foreword only deepens my regard for her; and finally, Christopher Gilbert, my then-fiancé-now-husband, whose faithful willingness to read, edit, and discuss each chapter as I wrote it was an invaluable gift and a much appreciated act of love. I have to believe that the one who prepares the eternal banquet is downright pleased with the kindnesses these folks have thrown my way. And I suspect he's cooking up something real good as a result!

1

"Pass Me the Balance"

Good, the more
Communicated, more abundant grows.
JOHN MILTON, PARADISE LOST, BOOK IV

In the 1970s, a radical movement swept the nation. It happened really because of the 1960s, an age that did not just
produce free love, rock and roll, and flower children. Many
formerly doped-up young people were finding peace and
love in something far beyond their antiwar demonstrations
and Woodstock passions. Instead of tripping on acid, they
were encountering the drama of the Book of books. Instead
of singing Bob Dylan and Janis Joplin songs, they were

15

singing upbeat hymns and spiritual choruses. Instead of protesting the establishment, they were passing out religious tracts to other teens and twenty-somethings. These young people searched for significance with perhaps more zeal and tenacity than any other younger generation in our country's history. But when all was said and done, what did they find? Simply put: Jesus. And though skeptics at first mocked the Jesus Movement as a mere reaction to the other highs of the sixties, thousands and thousands of young people knew that what they experienced was not just another trip. For many, they had come face to face with the living, moving God of history through the person of Jesus Christ. And their lives were never the same.

What happened, then, in many suburbs of the 1970s was a direct result of this Jesus Movement that had begun the decade before. These former hippies now were leading Bible studies and discipleship groups. They were concocting unconventional strategies to reach young people and, in the process, infusing new life into old missions. Peculiar new terms like "youth ministry" and "relationship evangelism" began popping up all over suburban high schools.

Mine was one of them.

I don't know if Chuck, Mary, and Maureen had been flower children or radicals; I just knew they ran one of these strange youth organizations that had grown out of the sixties' movement and into my suburban existence. My older brother attended their weekly meetings, and I figured if he could go, so could I. Besides, some of the cool kids at our high school were attending, and so I, out of my insecure adolescent drive for acceptance, decided this would be the place for me. My teenage life was a basket of extreme emotions, and I yearned (like those sixties' young people) for some sort of significance and meaning. What I hadn't counted on was what—or whom—I would discover at that youth gathering.

The winter of my sophomore year I accepted the invitation to become what others told me was called a Christian. My family had gone to church only sporadically, so I was not exactly sure about this Christianity stuff that I was getting into. I did know that my leaders' consistent portrayal of this man Jesus Christ was immensely attractive to me. Where before I had felt like an outsider, I now felt included. Before I had little sense of self-worth, now I felt valued. God loved *me*, they said—and that was no small thing to a teenage American girl. I spent my remaining high school years attending Bible studies, playing guitar for junior high kids' rallies, and trying to attain some sense of balance and consistency in my young Christian life.

I was not very good at it. By college I became disillusioned and restless. Still, I tried often to inject my spiritual veins with some sense of Christian enthusiasm by attending various activities, church events, and fellowship groups. But by graduation, I was well on my way to living a chaotic, peaceless life, albeit one full of nice Christian values. I got a job teaching English at another suburban high school and tried with sixties-style zeal to change the public school system with my crusading Christian witness. But I had one major problem: I wasn't balanced. My life was frantic, busy, and going in too many directions. How could I help anyone else grow in their faith if mine was so inconsistent, like a pendulum swinging from wall to wall?

When I finally stopped and listened to God six years later, I began to realize something had to give in order for me to live a healthy, vibrant, balanced life with the Jesus of my youth. Somehow I knew that an active, radical, and abundant life could only be nurtured by a solid, rejuvinating relationship with the Almighty. I began to see that a balanced life did not mean a passive, mundane, or hurried one. If anything, the life that Christ lived on earth was quite the opposite. Through a series of small, challenging

17

steps, I began to watch God's peaceful character and heart for order invade mine. Something was changing.

Eventually, my journey led me to enjoy the diversity of urban living, and I began teaching a college and career Sunday school class at the church I was attending. One morning, my bright twenty-something students looked me straight in the eye and asked with great seriousness how they could stay solid and on track in their Christian lives. They had watched too many of their friends fall from grace and were afraid they might do the same. They had witnessed too many Christian leaders fall dismally into sin and become public spectacles as a result. They were busy doing great things for God, alive with questions, and zealous (like I had been at their age), wanting to make an impact on their world. They wanted to know how to do more than merely survive; they—like all of us—wanted to live well, to enjoy an unmovable feast. So they wanted to know, how did I keep the faith without wavering, how did I stay consistent in a world that was always changing?

Were they talking to *me?!*

Their question forced me to take a long look at my own search for balance, one full of shortcomings, failures, and hard lessons. I had to look hard at what had kept me in this Christianity stuff, why I persevered with Jesus. As I did, I began to wonder why no one had taught me (or why I hadn't listened if they did) some basic principles for staying balanced and focused in the Christian life. Though many fine people have planted good seeds in my life, it has been my own spiritual stumbling along the way that has helped me understand a bit of what it means to walk without falling, how to keep my footing when the earth seems to be spinning so fast.

When these intelligent young Christians wanted to know how they could best apply their faith to their lives while remaining balanced in a world gone awry, I had to pay attention. They wanted practical guidelines for healthy living; they wanted time-tested principles that would keep them unmovable at the Christian feast. Consequently, on Sunday mornings for several months in a row, we set out to discover how we could remain balanced and effective Christians in a seemingly chaotic world.

What happened became the basis for this book.

Make a list of all the roles you play on a regular basis. This will help you assess the direction(s) and demands of your life.

Sick Faith

Unfortunately, along the journey I've met few people who lived as "well" as those youth leaders who changed my life. Too often, I see Christians (like me) who struggle daily just to stay afloat. Sure, our lives are full and busy, but we seem exhausted, cranky, and, sometimes, even out of control. We get stressed out, fed up, and worn down, emotionally, physically, and spiritually. Sadly, some of us even end up either burning out from all our spiritual activities or giving up on a God whom we bitterly believe has failed us.

It is a familiar story. Either people we've loved, or we ourselves, drop out of the race entirely because the pace of life becomes too much to bear. When this happens, some might argue whether our faith was ever real to begin with. No, I think most of us who call ourselves Christians are genuinely trying to love Jesus Christ. Others might say it is some unconfessed sin that brings on health problems or crises of faith. Maybe, but I think most of us sincerely want to live a life that pleases God. The plain and simple reason many Christians fall out of their relationship with Christ is that they're just not getting enough helpings—or the right kinds—of spiritual nourishment. So their bodies, and their faith, get . . . tired and sick.

All of us understand what it's like to feel undernourished, overextended, and out of balance. We go in too many directions and, as a result, aren't able to live well in any one. With this kind of pace, something is bound to snap. Our bodies just aren't meant to jump tall buildings in single bounds or race locomotives, though most of us believe we can. It doesn't help that we live in a country that sells busyness as the way to success. Yes, we need challenges to spur us on, diversity to keep life interesting. But A. W. Tozer put it well: "The simplicity which is in Christ is rarely found among us. In its stead are programs, methods, organizations, and a world of nervous activities which occupy time and attention, but can never satisfy the longing of the heart."

Let's face it: Many of us fill our lives with "nervous activities" that can never "satisfy the longing of the heart." What happens as a result? We get so busy looking spiritual that we neglect our solitude with God. Or we become so immersed in our community relationships that we forgo the nourishment of individual contemplation. Or we serve and give of ourselves until we collapse from exhaustion, feeling discouraged, hopeless, and far from God. When our lives run out of control, how can we expect to be anything but spiritually sick?

As simplistic as it sounds, my Sunday school students and I began to recognize that the demise of a person's spiritual health, or anyone who feels out of balance, can be compared to a person's daily eating habits. Since kindergarten, most North Americans have been taught that we need four basic food groups to provide us a healthy, balanced diet. Fruits and vegetables give us vitamins that build our immune system. Breads and grains provide our necessary carbohydrates. Dairy products make our bones strong, and the protein from meats or meat substitutes gives us energy. If we forsake any of these food groups, our teachers told us, we risk losing our health. In short, we get sick.

Likewise, we need regular helpings of four spiritual foods to keep our faith strong and to build in us a resistance to "otherworldly" illnesses. We need the nourishment of spiritual vitamins and nutrients to keep sin from penetrating our souls and to keep us persevering in the work God has given us each to do. In other words, we need a balanced, proactive spiritual diet to equip us for the abundant life God has called us to and to keep us from compromising our walk with him.

Finding a Balance

But that's not easy, we all know. My Oxford English Dictionary defines balance as, "to bring to or keep in equilibrium, to poise, keep steady, to equal; general harmony between the parts of anything." It is *not* passive or indifferent. Though my youth leaders showed me a positive example of coming to Christian faith, I have always struggled to learn what it means to stay in it, to "keep in equilibrium" the general parts of my life, and to retain a "steady" Christlike lifestyle in a world desperately in need of the hope of God's equalizing and transforming love. Like most Christians, I've felt the real tension between seeking God and seeking my own aspirations, between denying my self and loving my self. I have read plenty of books and magazines, listened to many sermons, attended countless Bible studies, and talked with numerous Christians about how in the world (and I mean that quite literally) we stay balanced and consistent in the midst of seemingly chaotic and busy lives. I've asked friends how they stay balanced, and they've told me things like, "The only way to catch up is to slow down"; "I breathe deeply, read *The New York Times*, and exercise"; or "I retreat to my 'silent cave' and wrestle with God." I know a balanced, vibrant life beats the alternative, but how do I get there?

"Help me, Jesus!" I plead.

As a journalist, I have covered conferences, interviewed leaders, and reported on events in the evangelical world over the past eight years, hoping also to find clues. Instead, I have listened to too many tales of a pastor's descent from faith, heard too many stories of ministries "going out of business," and read too many accounts of how ineffective the Christian church has been in reaching the American culture for Christ. It seems ours is a Christianity that has borne little fruit in the decades since the Jesus Movement. One need only look at current sociological statistics— divorce rates, teen pregnancies, crime statistics are higher than ever recorded in our country's history—to know how little our corporate faith has affected our culture. Even a Christian value system seems to know little influence in contemporary society.

Yes, we human beings are born into a spiritual tension between evil and good. Every person struggles daily with the decision of who will govern his life: self or God. Caught in this mass of flesh and bones is a strange paradox: We are fallen creatures, prone to sin, born with evil, deceptive hearts, yet created in the image of God! We are not, in and of ourselves, good, as some would like to think. Besides the horrors throughout history that prove our innate evil, we need only look at the nature of every child and know that no parent has to teach him to be bad!

Thankfully, though, we are not just wretched worms that wander aimlessly throughout a miserable existence.

We are also heavenly creations made in God's image, designed to worship him with all of our lives. The Latin concept *imago Dei*, which means in the image of God, is true for us daily, and his redemptive purposes have a wonderful "habit" of turning our wormlike ways to good. This, of course, is more powerful than the forces of evil that roam the world in acts of selfishness, abuse, and violence.

Even so, it is still a wonder to me when absolute strangers help each other by holding open a door, or hammering a nail on a Habitat for Humanity house. I am amazed when a symphony plays, a child reads aloud, a neighbor bakes cookies for me, or a teenager in this day of relative values and comfortable beliefs takes a stand for his Christian beliefs in a public school. In essence, there is too much good still in this sometimes maddening world to think the Almighty has stopped working, if even anonymously.

The reality, though, is we all live with tension, struggle, conflict. Every day. If we are honest with ourselves, we know how tough it is to let right win over wrong. It is difficult to pursue a life of integrity and goodness when we are enticed constantly with temporary, worldly pleasures. We all have watched mature Christians turn away from God when the changes of life or the consequences of their choices became too difficult to bear. Even the great apostle Paul faced the battle between sin and righteousness when he wrote, "I know that nothing good lives in me, that is, in my sinful nature. For I have the desire to do what is good, but I cannot carry it out. For what I do is not the good I want to do; no, the evil I do not want to do—this I keep on doing" (Rom. 7:18–19).

How does Romans 7:18–19 apply to you right now?

23

An Age of *Progress?*

And so I ask, like my students did, "How can I live for Christ in such a difficult time as this, without falling away or succumbing to indifference? How can I keep centered when my schedule becomes so demanding? How can I keep a balanced, loving perspective when evil runs rampant around me?" I know I need balance, that is, an active radical discipleship, if I am going to stand firm in my relationship with God and with others. I know I need an anchor to keep me from drifting away from the faith that has literally changed my life. Yet, in an age of dysfunctional families, information overload, sociopathic violence, and systemic racism, I often feel overwhelmed and discouraged. Ours is a world that seems out of control. Chaos, disorder, and overstimulation have become as normal as peaceful Sundays used to be.

Progress has not necessarily helped us either. Though we have bigger, faster gadgets to bring us more convenience and comfortableness, they have not really helped our quality of life. If anything, they've inundated our lives with more information than we can possibly absorb in a lifetime. I read in a magazine recently that more information has been generated in the last three decades than in the previous five thousand years. Over four thousand books are published every day. One weekday edition of *The New York Times* includes more information than the average person encountered in his entire lifetime in seventeenth-century England! They've flooded us with choices that only feed our greedy natures and made the modern U.S. resident virtually inept at taking care of himself and our planet without electricity, microwaves, cars, or technological equipment, not to mention the way these devices drive us away from what once was considered quality time with others. North Americans produce literally tons of garbage yearly, and for every ton of waste at the consumer end, another five tons of waste is required from the manufacturing stage. Yes, we have more stuff to make life easier than ever before, but considering we boast some of the highest statistics in cancer, heart disease, divorce, crime, and drug abuse in the world, I'm not sure our technological advances have advanced us at all!

Anthropologists have long pointed out that despite all the American hoopla about progress, the truth is the more "primitive" a culture, the more leisured its people are in its ways of life. Early settlers in Maryland, for instance, often marveled that many Indians were great-grandfathers, while in England, few people survived to become grandparents. Many original documents of settlers and explorers observe that natives in the Pacific Islands, Australia, the Americas, and the Middle East enjoyed longer, healthier lives than did their foreign, civilized counterparts.

Perhaps that's why contemporary British journalist Malcolm Muggeridge, who came to Christian faith late in his life, made the following observation:

> I disbelieve in progress, the pursuit of happiness, and all the concomitant notions and projects for creating a society in which human beings find ever greater contentment by being given in ever greater abundance the means to satisfy their material and bodily hopes and desires. . . . The half century in which I have been consciously alive seems to me to have been quite exceptionally destructive, murderous, and brutal. More people have been killed and terrorized, more driven from their homes and native places, more of the past's heritage has been destroyed, more lies propagated and base persuasion engaged in, with less compensatory achievement in art, literature, and imaginative understanding, than in any comparable period of history.[1]

How, then, do we keep our balance when our "progressive" world seems to be spinning out of control? I believe we can only turn to the words of Psalm 121: "I lift up my eyes to the hills—where does my help come from? My help comes from the LORD, the Maker of heaven and earth. He will not let your foot slip—he who watches over you will not slumber" (vv. 1–3). Yes! For the Christian who is confident of God's sovereignty and grace, who knows intimately the Maker of both a jubilant heaven and this crazy earth, there is hope. There is a confidence in knowing he will not let our foot slip. I'm convinced of it.

Reflect on Psalm 121 for a moment. How might it relate to Romans 7:18–19?

Changing Our Diet

Before long in our class, I began to recognize what a healthy spiritual diet needed to include. I valued *solitude*, that is, individual time spent daily with Jesus worshiping, praying, and reading his Word. As the great African church father St. Augustine said, "Our hearts are restless until they find rest in You alone, oh, God." But I knew I could not stay on a mountaintop in the presence of God alone: I needed to serve others just as much as I needed to be alone with God. *Service* became an integral outflow of exercising my faith.

Yet, if I served apart from being in *community* or in fellowship with other Christians, I could burn out quickly and become bitter. The German World War II martyr Dietrich Bonhoeffer understood this when he wrote in his book *Life Together*, "The prisoner, the sick person, the Christian exile sees in the companionship of a fellow Christian a physical sign of the gracious presence of the triune God."[2] Likewise, I needed the refreshment and encouragement of the saints to keep me pressing on.

I also realized that I could not merely thrive on solitude, service, and community: I needed continually to renew my mind and be *contemplative*. By study, discussion, reflection, and the arts, my mind would remain active and guarded against the world's constant bombardment of distractions. The Bible is full of admonitions to meditate on the works of the Lord, to consider his greatness, to remember his acts of kindness, and to think on that which is excellent and praiseworthy. Our minds matter in living out our faith.

So a balanced Christian life is one that models the life of Christ and includes consistent portions of solitude, service, community, and contemplation. These anchor us for abundant daily living, a life that is both peaceful and pleasing to God. As our group discussed what I came to call the "Four spiritual food groups for living a balanced Christian life," we became better equipped to maintain a steady, enthusiastic relationship with the Maker of heaven and earth. We also saw that regardless of personality type or temperament, these four spiritual food groups could help any Christian who wanted to live a balanced, sensitive life with his or her Creator.

Briefly define in your own words solitude, service, community, and contemplation.

We talked about how we need to retreat in solitude for our bread and water, to refresh, rebuild, and recharge our relationship with the triune God. We distinguished between the attitude and the actions of a servant, and how service best reflects the lifestyle of Christ working in us. We confessed that we could not function well or effectively apart from each other; we needed the community of each other (the body of believers) to encourage, challenge, comfort, and protect us. And in the midst of each, we determined the importance of renewing our minds, meditating on and contemplating truth through Scripture, teachings, discussions, books, and the arts.

Then a wonderful thing occurred: These young Christians began to teach each other the importance of integrating these spiritual foods into their lives on a regular basis. In fact, I often heard them keeping each other accountable whenever they felt out of balance. They met regularly for prayer, Bible study, and social gatherings to build community. They looked for ways to serve each other and their city. They passed around books they were reading, and one time I even overheard one woman ask another, "You seem tired from your busy schedule. Are you getting enough solitude or contemplation?"

Artificial Flavorings

During our study, however, we also discovered that these four spiritual foods could take on counterfeit forms. For instance, one could spend so much time alone and apart from the accountability and support of others, that he or she could become a reclusive, self-absorbed hermit who has no impact on the world. To stay apart and away from others too much is to nurture selfish insecurities and inappropriate attitudes.

Or we could pursue the wrong type of community. All humans, of course, have a need for belonging, companionship, and affirmation. Many today find it in bars, support groups, work, health clubs, or teams, where they often become susceptible to unhealthy codependent relationships. What happens is that instead of relying on the source or the head of the body—God himself—to meet our needs, we run the risk of romanticizing the power of the other, putting unrealistic expectations and pressures on friends to provide for our emotional longings. Interdependent community relationships are necessary, but they are only healthy and biblical when the individuals are looking first to God to fulfill them and meet their needs.

Likewise, those who seek to serve for the sake of their own satisfaction often become trapped in a counterfeit form of service. We know the type: "I gave food to the homeless and it made me feel so good that I could help them." "I like helping these poor inner-city kids; they don't have anyone who cares about them like I do." This patronizing, self-aggrandizing response does little to actually help anyone—including those doing the helping—because it thwarts a mutual exchange of dignity, the very definition of Christian service.

And, of course, we can get so intellectual and academic from all our studying and contemplating that we are no earthly good, the final counterfeit. We forget to feel, forget that to be human is also to have emotions, passions, and a sense of wonder. For instance, I had a friend once whose counselor told him he had a problem with intimacy in relationships. Instead of talking with other friends to help him through it, he went to the library, checked out eight books on intimacy, and read every one, thinking an intellectual understanding alone would solve his problem with relationships!

Healthy "Eating"

So we must be careful. These four spiritual food groups can be easily disguised. But of equal caution, I must note

29

that when any one authentic group is missing from our spiritual diet, we will inevitably feel out of balance, chaotic, or exhausted. We might even set ourselves up to sin or displease God. That is why solitude, service, community, and contemplation are all equally important; all four provide nourishment for the whole feast called life.

I also firmly believe that fundamental attributes of the Christian life (or nutrients for the sake of the analogy), that is, prayer, worship, fasting, evangelism, confession, and celebration, are inherent elements of each spiritual food group. For example, we can pray or study with other Christians in community, fast and worship during times of solitude, evangelize and pray as we serve, and confess or celebrate as we contemplate the Scriptures.

Obviously, regular helpings of these four spiritual food groups will only work if we work; in and of themselves, they cannot guarantee that every sheep will keep from wandering away from the flock. Certainly, spiritual balance is no easy task given our spinning world and our paradoxical nature. But I do believe that these four attributes, as we discuss them throughout these next pages, best reflect the lifestyles of those women and men throughout the Scriptures, history, and contemporary life who most consistently, powerfully, and humbly understood what it meant to walk with God until he called them home to his eternal banquet. They are the keys to living a balanced, fulfilling life.

If we will value solitude, service, community, and contemplation, keeping them as regular priorities in our lives, developing them as habits like we would eating the right foods, then I believe our lives will be perpetually abundant and full, looking more and more like the one whose life, death, and resurrection changed history, and is changing you and me.

"We have this hope as an anchor for the soul, firm and secure" (Heb. 6:19).

Spend a few minutes in prayer,
reflecting on Hebrews 6:19.
Give thanks to God for the ways
your Anchor has kept you
from drifting.

2

SOLITUDE:
BREAKFAST WITH JESUS

The happiest of all lives is a busy solitude.
VOLTAIRE, LETTER TO FREDERICK THE GREAT,
AUGUST 1751

Several years ago, I was visiting some old college friends and their children. It was a time to catch up with these friends and get reacquainted with their youngsters. While their mother and father were cooking dinner, I followed the three children into their family room to play with them.

But three-year-old Rachel didn't seem to care that her siblings had chosen a cartoon video as their source of entertainment. She had suddenly found another source of fascinating amusement: my face.

This little girl kneeled on my lap, her big brown eyes only inches from mine, searching every part of my face. Her tiny hands pushed part of my cheek or jaw into strange shapes, and she giggled and laughed until she discovered another shape. When this became dull, she traced my eyebrows and forehead with her index finger and giggled again. No matter what her strategy, for fifteen minutes straight her face never turned from mine. No matter how loud her brother and sister got, no matter what happened in the video, Rachel's attention was not diverted. She was intent—for some strange reason—on studying my face.

If ever there was a grand image of what our relationship with God could look like, Rachel showed it to me that day she became infatuated with my face. In the same way, we need to learn to "get into God's face," tracing his eyebrows, squeezing his cheeks until we giggle and laugh and know what he looks like. We must not allow our attention to be diverted; instead we need to develop a "childlike" intensity for gazing on the face of God.

As we seek to balance our lives and enjoy his unmovable feast, the first place we must go is to God. And we must go in solitude. Regardless of the demands of our days or the pressures we feel from relationships, it is crucial for the Christian to retreat regularly to meet with her God. Lonely, quiet places away paradoxically fill us with joy and peace; they renew our souls and restore our focus. And so solitude is the first source of nourishment in our four spiritual food groups because it rewards us with energy and strength to return to the tasks we have been given to do.

Describe the place or places where you regularly meet with God in solitude. If you don't have one, think of a quiet, lonely place where you could go.

Solitary Fellowship

When I looked in my Oxford English Dictionary for the historic meaning of the word *solitude*, I couldn't help but notice the many other words that have the prefix *soli*. Solid is "free from empty spaces, cavities, etc., having the interior completely filled in or up; of a strong, firm, or substantial nature or quality; not slight or flimsy." Solidarity is "the fact or quality on the part of communities of being perfectly united or at one in some respect." Solidify is "to make firm, hard or compact." Solitary is "one who retires into, or lives in, solitude from religious motives; a hermit or recluse; one who is deprived of the society of others."

The Latin derivation for solitude is *solitas*, which means simply "loneliness or being alone." And the actual definition for solitude is "the state of being or living alone; loneliness, seclusion, solitariness of persons; loneliness of places; remoteness from habitations; absence of life or stir; a complete absence or lack." A simple study of these words can provide us with a number of insights about the need for and fruit of solitude.

When we make intentional time for solitude, that is, when we put ourselves in a secluded, lonely, remote habitation, one absent of stir, a strange thing occurs. We set our face to no other distractions but the face of God. We look to him. As we do, our spiritual character becomes solid: The interior is

35

completely filled up and made strong, firm, and substantial. We develop a solidarity with God, the Triune Person magnified in the Father, Son, and Holy Spirit, becoming united with his heart, perspective, and being. His truth is solidified in us, made firm and hard, and we begin to crave again more solitary times, where we are purposely deprived of the society of others and are so infatuated (which means "to inspire with foolish passion or love") with the face of God through our solitude that we will want to forsake the ways of the world to be alone with him. His presence and his astounding love will capture our hearts, and we will find time spent with him as captivating as Rachel did with my face.

In solitude with God, convictions are solidified, visions instilled, faith enlarged, and integrity born and built. Inevitably, these become a fortress of protection when we reenter the world and are faced with numerous temptations or opportunities to compromise our faith. What happens in solitude always affects what happens outside it. The person who does not nurture this time is much more susceptible to falling into sin or losing his balance. Why? He has not built up his spiritual defenses in the gift of solitude.

Spend a few silent moments now asking God to birth in you integrity and to increase your faith. You might want to reflect on Luke 17:5–6.

One Fine Fish Fry

One of my favorite stories in the Bible is in John 21:1–14 when Jesus cooks breakfast for the disciples. His interaction with his disciples was one of many instances when he appeared *after* his atoning death on the cross. In other words, he had already risen from the grave and now wanted to spend a little more time with his followers to encourage them in their faith.

Imagine the scene: You have just watched the only person who has ever offered you hope die a grueling death from an atrocious execution of beatings, blood, and mockery. You know he is dead; you watched with your own eyes as he gasped for his last breath. You are sure he is gone. You try to work through the pain and loss by spending time with your friends. You meet in the home of one of your friends, doors locked in case the local authorities are looking for you. Together, you grieve and talk quietly and painfully of the man you lost on the cross, the man who had promised you life and hope and was murdered before your eyes because of it.

Then he appears. Walks right through the locked door and says, "Peace be with you." You rub your eyes, certain your grief has become so overwhelming that now you are seeing things. But you aren't, and you hear it again. "Peace be with you!" It is your Hope, come back to encourage you, to wipe your tears, to give you comfort and purpose and forgiveness. He does incredible things in front of you and your friends, miracles even, so that your heart will be full of faith and trust to prepare you for the future, the time long after you see his body, when you will know, in spite of what others will say, he is alive.

Days later, he is gone. Again. You feel alone again so you decide together to go fishing; it was what you used to do to earn a living before this man changed your life. Besides, you need to eat, you tell yourself. You set out on the sea, but the fish aren't biting at all. It feels like nature's cruel joke. You feel the lump from deep in your soul rise up within you, and the tears start spilling down your face.

Then all of a sudden some guy from the shore begins to yell at you, asking if you've caught anything. Is he kidding? No, you snap back, embarrassed and distraught. He then suggests you throw your net on the right side of the boat. Yeah, right, you think. But at this point, what have you got to lose? You cast your nets over on the right side, and before you know it, you have lots and lots of fish, 153 to be exact. Your eyes have witnessed another miracle, and when you look at the man on the shore you realize it is your Hope. Again. Alive, in human flesh, standing there by a fire of burning coals with fish already sizzling on it, holding some bread, smiling probably. It is the Lord Jesus, and what does he do next? He says, "Come and have breakfast" (v. 12).

The fact that the Gospel writer even included this simple invitation to "Come and have breakfast" is a beautiful picture of God's invitation to fellowship with him. Why? Because still he makes us breakfast. Though daily we might forget (like the disciples did) that Jesus Christ is alive, that he is able to do far more than we ask or imagine as the apostle Paul wrote in Ephesians 3:20, he invites us to a feast that he personally is preparing. Though we might mope around in our distress and try to fill up our lives with diversions, he calls us to come away, to come and eat with him. In fact, he even offers to do the cooking! This is the call to solitude, to time spent in his presence, where the fire is already burning and he is waiting.

Write down what it must have felt like being on the shore with Jesus after his death, now watching him fry fish for you.

Laying the Foundation

When the century's greatest British apologist, C. S. Lewis, first acknowledged Christ's invitation, he walked slowly, reluctantly even, toward the fire. He had been a devoted philosophy and literature student with little time for thoughts of God. Foolishness, he called it. Yet, his academic pursuits could not deafen the call he heard again and again from the man on the shore:

> You must picture me alone in that room in Magdalen (College), night after night, feeling, whenever my mind lifted even for a second from my work, the steady, unrelenting approach of Him whom I so earnestly desired not to meet. That which I greatly feared had at last come upon me. In the Trinity Term of 1929 I gave in, and admitted that God was God, and knelt and prayed: perhaps, that night, the most dejected and reluctant convert in all England. I did not then see what is now the most shining and obvious thing: the Divine humility which will accept a convert even on such terms. The Prodigal Son at least walked home on his own feet. But who can duly adore that Love which will open the high gates to a prodigal who is brought in kicking, struggling, resentful, and darting his eyes in every direction for a chance to escape? The words *compelle intrare*, compel them to come in, have been so abused by wicked men that we shudder at them; but, properly understood, they plumb the depth of the Divine mercy. The hardness of God is kinder than the softness of men, and His compulsion is our liberation.[1]

Doesn't Lewis beautifully describe the person who captured even "a dejected convert's" attention, leaving him no alternative but to accept the invitation to come? Though for him it was the first time he acknowledged divine mercy, we all know that the "kicking, struggling, resentment and search for an escape" don't stop even after we've "admitted that God is God." The effort to nurture a solitary fellow-ship is a continual, difficult process; it is indeed the heart of the Christian walk. Yet, what a liberating joy to partake of the kindness of God, to experience a "love which will open the high gates" for us; certainly that is the sure foundation from which we must build our lives of faith.

So the call of Jesus from the shore to come to him was for two reasons: He loved being with the disciples, and he knew they needed to be with him. As Lewis discovered, being together was for their own good, so he could continue to form in them that which would please him most: his character. (See Heb. 13:21.) In the same way, we are molded into his likeness as we sit with him. It is much like the process of raising a child. Consider how a parent invests (or should anyway) countless hours in a child's self-esteem and moral character at home, teaching her the differences between right and wrong, how to respect authority, and the virtues of honesty and self-discipline. As the child learns these from a parent—who is equally lavishing her with love and affirmation—the less likely she is to give way to peer pressure. When the temptations, for example, of sexual immorality or drug abuse are thrown her way—as they will inevitably be, given the reality of our society—she will likely be able to withstand them because she has been taught at home that those things are not right, nor are they good for her. She trusts that her father or mother told her the right thing.

I believe it is the same for us as children of God. When we spend time with him, God's character—his value system if you will—is formed in us. This is where our identity is formed, where our security takes root. Indeed, it is in this consistent exchange with the Father that the confidence of a child is developed. We learn to listen to his words of encouragement and love as we read the Bible, which, in turn, shape our attitudes toward ourselves and the lens through which we see the world.

40

The Bible compares this to the building of a house. In Luke 6:46–49, Jesus challenges his disciples:

> Why do you call me, "Lord, Lord," and do not do what I say? I will show you what he is like who comes to me and hears my words and puts them into practice. He is like a man building a house, who dug down deep and laid the foundation on rock. When a flood came, the torrent struck that house but could not shake it, because it was well built. But the one who hears my words and does not put them into practice is like a man who built a house on the ground without a foundation. The moment the torrent struck that house, it collapsed and its destruction was complete.

Notice how Jesus first challenges his hearers to take seriously their relationship with him as Lord, to "do what I say." Then he defines what solitude is: "he . . . who comes to me and hears my words and puts them into practice." The balanced believer comes to Jesus regularly, hears his words and allows them to change him, to flow out of him into a lifestyle that looks like Christ's. When he does, he has built his house—his very dwelling place—on a rock that cannot be shaken regardless of the circumstances. The one who calls Christ "Lord" digs down deep to lay his foundation; he is serious, disciplined, and enthusiastic in his building because he knows that this is the only thing that can save him when the floods hit. Solitude with God prepares us for any storms that might come our way.

Consider how you've built your spiritual "house." Is it built on shaky ground or on the rock of Christ? How can you build on him?

But we also see from this parable what happens when we don't take time to be with God: It "is like a man who built a house on the ground without a foundation. The moment the torrent struck that house, it collapsed and its destruction was complete" (Luke 6:49). Sadly, too many of us go through the motions of a Christian lifestyle without the life-sustaining relationship with Christ himself. Sure, we might be guided by Christian values, but when the torrent strikes, when the challenges come, we collapse in our shaky beliefs and insecurities. In other words, a nice value system is not enough to sustain us during difficult times; we have to nurture an ongoing, vibrant friendship with the living person of God himself, a God who deeply desires our fellowship.

We also need to consider how we derive our sense of security and stability. Do we build on God's enduring words of truth or on what we hear during our interactions with the world? Unfortunately, too many of us work for attention and affirmation by *doing*, rather than by simply accepting the love of the Father in our *being*. And certainly it is easy to understand why: We live in a society in which our identity is usually based on what we do. At a gathering at which we're meeting people for the first time, for instance, the subject of what we do vocationally is usually the very next piece of information we offer after we introduce ourselves: "Hi, I'm Jo. I'm a teacher and a writer." Or "I'm Jody. I'm a nurse." Or "I'm Daniel. I'm an actor." Too often we allow our professions to define us as we live in a culture that also categorizes those careers. The more prestigious an individual's job, the more "important" he is. Those who don't earn much money (and therefore fame) in their careers never receive VIP status, that is, are rarely perceived as a "very important person."

All of our doing or performing in our careers, even in our "ministries," can lead to false securities and eventually, burnout. But let's remember Jesus' words about the one who builds a balanced, sturdy house: "I will show you what he is like who comes to me and hears my words and puts them into practice" (Luke 6:47). He comes to *me*, Jesus says. That's the first step; then the doing happens. When we find our identity and security—the very essence of who we are—in the immense love of God, the love that Psalm 103:11 says is "as high as the heavens are above the earth," then we can serve and work and do, not to gain God's attention, but because we have received a gracious gift from him and want genuinely to give back.

Reflect on—or sing—the old children's song "Jesus Loves Me." Let its truth settle into your soul right now.

Proactive Places

But solitude is not exactly easy to achieve on a regular basis, especially since the world is a busier, more populated, and increasingly stimulated place than at any other time in history. We have more technological distractions and hurried paces than ever before; retreating from the rushed neon life of Western society is no easy task. No wonder Oswald Chambers said, "Solitude with God repairs the damage done by the fret and noise and clamour of the world."

I have a friend who learned this the hard way. He was newly married, working two part-time jobs, pastoring a small church in an urban neighborhood, and going to graduate school. If he wasn't writing a paper or driving to work, he was leading a Bible study or helping a parishioner find a job. His busy schedule never included rest or quiet retreating, yet he always seemed to be excited about all the things "God was doing" in his life.

But eventually the "doings" caught up with him, threw him into a clinical depression, and he withdrew from every part of his life. For months, his wife did not even know where he was. Finally, he took several small steps to recover from the intense pressures that came from ignoring the call to solitude, and today, after five years of incredible pain, medical treatment, and spiritual counsel, he is realizing the need to slow down. He has even scheduled regular times of solitary reflection, prayer, and rest into his weekly commitments.

We mustn't let our lifestyles become so out of control that we are literally forced to retreat. Hopefully, we can see that the invitation to come away needs to be proactive, rather than reactive, like it was for my friend. Remember how our mothers taught us to eat all four food groups regularly so we wouldn't get sick? We shouldn't change our diets *after* we have a heart attack; we should stop eating fried and high fat foods to prevent us from having one. Our spiritual balance operates on the same principle.

Obviously, we need God through his Holy Spirit to bring us to a lonely, "called-out" place. We need him to help us be still *before* life gets so noisy and cluttered that we crack from the pressure. We need him to show us the power of being quiet in the presence of the one who is in the business of changing our lives. As Henri J. Nouwen rightly called it, "Solitude is the furnace of transformation but you do not make it happen. God does."[2] The consuming fire of God's presence certainly burns away all that needs changing in us, but like the coals Jesus used to cook the fish, it also can be used to nourish and strengthen us for what he's called us to be and do. Happily, his compulsion is our liberation, as Lewis said.

The Productivity of Rest

In music, a rest is not idleness; it is waiting to come in again. That is exactly how we should view our solitary fellowship, our godly rest; it is simply time apart during which we gain refreshment and wait to come back into the world again. Unfortunately, too many of us feel guilty if we lie on the couch some Sunday afternoon, when we really should be out working in the garden. Or if we just sit quietly at home Wednesday night with a book, we can't enjoy it because we think we should be at the midweek church service. Or if we take a Saturday morning to sleep in and plan nothing, we perceive ourselves as lazy—or think others will see us that way.

No, I know very few friends who see rest as a productive, necessary aspect to living a balanced life. With good reason. Many in the evangelical community think we must be going a hundred miles an hour all the time to be productive; there are, after all, souls to be saved, sermons to be preached, hearts to be won, worlds to be changed. Those things are certainly true and important. Yet, if God didn't think rest and solitude were a good idea, he himself would not have created the Sabbath or rested on the seventh day of creation. I doubt we would have seen the countless examples in Scripture where God's servants "went up on the mountain" to be with him. And I doubt we would have seen Jesus withdraw to the hills so often to pray.

Yes, we need to work for God, but I believe it is only fruitful for the kingdom if it is a natural outflow of our times spent alone in his presence. We must learn to "Be silent before the Sovereign LORD, for the day of the LORD is near. The LORD has prepared a sacrifice; he has consecrated those he has invited" (Zeph. 1:7).

Our hearts are changed and stilled from the busyness of life when we come quietly before God in prayer, study, and contemplation. When we build our spiritual foundation on his love, when we come into his presence of peace, when we sit quietly before the throne of grace, we are forming a protective, healing shield around us that will not fall when the waves strike against it. I like how the Catholic art critic Sister Wendy Beckett described it in her lovely book *Meditations on Silence:* "Entering into silence is like stepping into cool clear water. The dust and debris are quietly washed away, and we are purified of our triviality. This cleansing takes place whether we are conscious of it or not: the very choice of silence, of desiring to be still, washes away the day's grime."[3]

Yes, God desires our fellowship to wash us anew each day, to re-create his ways in us, and to remind us of his fatherly love for us. He wants us alone with him to wash away our daily grime and purify for himself a people "without spot or blemish." He wants us with him. Period. Because as John White describes it in his book *The Fight*, "Deep within your vast interior space is a tabernacle God built to commune with you. From it He calls you with tender urgency."[4]

Not long ago, I sat on the porch of a friend's house as I watched a small girl no older than five or six playing across the street. She did not see me, so she played without inhibition. Her thin brown hair blew around her face as she explored the wooded field that ran parallel to her house. Laughter rang from her belly as she picked wildflowers, skipped over puddles, or peeked under rocks. Then suddenly, the girl's attention became particularly focused; she had taken a big grey and black rock, bigger than both her hands put together, and forced it over, like a turtle turned on its back.

I have no idea what she discovered on the cold, dark dirt where the rock once lay, maybe a tiny snake, an assortment of bugs and spiders, or a rusted metal knife. Whatever she saw, though, sent terror through that little girl's body as she stood straight up, stiffened her shoulders, and froze. Her eyes grew bigger, and fear filled her face, but she could not move. Then a curious thing happened. She did not scream in a high-pitched shrill. She did not try to attack whatever was the source of her fear, stomp on it, or even put the rock back to pretend it didn't happen. She simply let out one heartfelt word with incredible confidence: "Mommmm-yyy!" And with that, her little legs let go of the fear and carried the child quickly back inside her house, in search of her mother's comfort.

I marveled at the wonderful assurance that little girl reflected both as she played and as she was frightened: She knew that her mother was never far from her and so she was safe. No matter what she might encounter, no matter what the situation might bring, this little girl had the security that her mother was close by to protect her, help her, even play with her. She did not try to conquer the fear on her own; rather she allowed the fear to send her to her source of help. I knew as I watched that such confidence did not just magically appear within the child; it had come no doubt because of many, many gentle interactions she had had with her parent, interactions that had built trust and assurance, confidence and security.

Certainly, God is calling each of us to recognize that he is never far off, that he desires his children to come and look close into his face. It will be a transforming gaze, to be sure, but one we cannot afford to do without—for our own sake and for the world's.

Have breakfast now with Jesus by reading silently Psalm 23. Let the Holy Spirit lead you beside still waters as he restores your soul in the quiet. Reflect on his love and character.

SOLITUDE:
SETTING THE TABLE FOR ONE

Teach us to care and not to care.
Teach us to sit still.
T. S. ELIOT, "ASH WEDNESDAY"

"That night Jacob got up and took his two wives, his two maidservants and his eleven sons and crossed the ford of the Jabbok. After he had sent them across the stream, he sent over all his possessions. So Jacob was left alone, and a man wrestled with him till daybreak. When the man saw that he could not overpower him, he touched the socket of

Jacob's hip so that his hip was wrenched as he wrestled with the man. Then the man said, 'Let me go, for it is daybreak.'

"But Jacob replied, 'I will not let you go unless you bless me.'

"The man asked him, 'What is your name?'

"'Jacob,' he answered.

"Then the man said, 'Your name will no longer be Jacob, but Israel, because you have struggled with God and with men and have overcome.'

"Jacob said, 'Please tell me your name.'

"But he replied, 'Why do you ask my name?' Then he blessed him there.

"So Jacob called the place Peniel, saying, 'It is because I saw God face to face, and yet my life was spared.'

"The sun rose above him as he passed Peniel, and he was limping because of his hip" (Gen. 32:22–31).

In the previous chapter, we discovered how God is calling us to come away to be with him, to form his character in us and to establish our security in his limitless love. We know why solitude is important and how much we need to nurture a solitary fellowship with the Creator of our hearts. But how in the world—and I mean that quite literally—do we get there?

Surely not the way Jacob did! His story is usually the last thing we want to think of when considering what solitude looks like. Let's be honest, most of us would rather not regard our relationship with God as a form of spiritual All Star Wrestling, if you will; instead, we want our quiet, devotional times to be nice fluffy moments with the Maker during which we unload all our problems on him, drink in a little of his unconditional love and acceptance, and go on our merry Christian way. We have done our duty after all, haven't we?

Though I suppose this type of "devotion" does have its place, I'm not so sure it provides the solidarity with God or spiritual sustenance we discussed earlier, a nourishment necessary for maintaining a balanced life of faith. We know God is calling us to set aside regular time with him to build our relationship, just as we would do to build a friendship or special relationship with a loved one. He longs for us to build our foundation on his grace, love, and unchanging Word. And we know we need it if we want to be solid reflections of hope in an often hopeless world. But with the number of constant distractions around us and with our own personal inconsistencies within us, we have to ask ourselves, Just how do we do that? How do we nurture solitary fellowship with the one who calls himself "I Am"? How do we set the table for one?

Imagine your ideal time of quiet and rest. Draw a picture of what it would look like or use words to describe each aspect of it.

The Jacob Principle

First, perhaps solitude requires us to rethink our perception of "quiet times." If solitary fellowship is anything, it is the Jacob in each of us wrestling with the divine Sovereign. When we're honest with ourselves, we realize it is really a battle of wills, a struggle for control, an exchange of tension. It is no small thing to sit still with the Almighty. Sure, we know (intellectually, at least) that it brings cleansing and healing for us, but it requires us to admit first and foremost, as Lewis said, that "God is God," a difficult confession for self-sufficient Westerners who like to run our own lives. Yet, before we even start the match, we know

51

who's going to win, and deep in our souls we are thankful for that reality. So we enter it anyway, knowing somehow that we cannot survive in this world unless we "wrestle" first with its Maker. Such an interaction, as we will see, requires unhurried, undistracted, alone time as well as tenacity and focus. Each yields an ongoing attitude of awareness—the goal of solitary fellowship. As a result, we receive blessing, identity, and vision.

Jacob's story provides some helpful insights of what it means to develop a perpetual attitude of solitary fellowship, or as the sixteenth-century monk Brother Lawrence called it, "practicing the presence of God." At first glance, we watch Jacob intentionally sending away his family for some time with God. Not that he didn't want to be with them; he was a respectable family man who took care of his own. But he was stressed at the moment, terrified that his big brother Esau (along with four hundred very macho warriors) was coming after him, about to do him in, intent on getting even with Jacob for what could be called a "sibling rivalry." "In great fear and distress," verse 7 says, this man of God even strategized how to protect most of his family in case Esau attacked them. Jacob had been known to talk often with God, and if ever he needed a healthy dose of fatherly inspiration, it was now.

He then got rid of any possible distractions by sending his possessions across the river. The text doesn't tell us whether Jacob knew what was about to happen, just that he seized the moment to be completely alone in the presence of one far greater than himself. So after every one was out of his hair and nothing was around to divert his attention, that's when (as some contemporary Christians like to say) God "showed up" and the games began. There was utter focus on the part of both "men," a motion of conflict and agony, one against the other; quite the opposite of, say, the motion of dancing in which two bodies work together gracefully. A neck hold, a body slam, a full nelson, who knows? But it was definitely a match in which will fought against Will. The man could easily have overpowered Jacob, but when he recognized Jacob's tenacity and his healthy fear of God, he responded graciously to the mere mortal beneath him: He touched (not struck or punched or slammed, but touched) his hip; it was wrenched, and the human was no doubt suddenly very aware of his frailty. Yet, even before Jacob fully recognized with whom he was fighting, his desperation turned into determination, and he refused to give up.

It was not as if the man could not break Jacob's hold when he said, "Let me go, for it is daybreak." Rather, he knew that Jacob's human eyes could not withstand the holy sight of God Incarnate. Jacob hung on anyway, pleading with the man to bless him, in spite of an excruciatingly painful hip and exhausted muscles. After the long, sweaty night of struggle, God not only blessed his chosen one, he gave him a new name, Israel, a new identity, a new sense of purpose. He was well aware of the plans he had for Jacob. And for us.

Often we don't know what to do when we are alone with God. Jacob's human instincts said to fight, and in so doing, he was humbled, blessed, changed, and strengthened in his spirit and vision. No doubt he limped that morning toward his family with new faith, new resilience that he would not be abandoned in spite of what the circumstances might bring. In losing his will to God, he won more than he could have imagined: his family's safety, a brother's forgiveness, and a people's God-ordained heritage. And everyone— from the Israelites of the Old Testament to the Christians of the 1990s—was affected as a result of his determination to be alone with God. Why? Because when we trace the genealogy of our Savior, it points several generations back to a man named Jacob whose identity and vision for his people were solidified during that painful night of encountering God.

And so it is with us as we cultivate solitary fellowship. The point of Jacob's story is not that we need to whip ourselves into spiritual shape by diving into the ring of some intense, all-night prayer punching. Though some of us might feel at times like we are indeed involved in a serious brawl with God, the message of Israel goes well beyond this. To live a balanced, consistent walk with the God of Israel, we must fight off distractions and cultivate an attitude of assurance that he is with us for the battles yet to come, determining "not to let go" of the King of Kings no matter how tired or hurt we might feel. Of the four spiritual food groups that help us gain and keep our balance, many Christians tell me solitude is the hardest to swallow. (Pun intended!) It is not easy, but it is crucial . . . for everyone's sake.

Get out your calendar and schedule in an appointment with God away from the daily responsibilities and diversions of life, maybe at a retreat center or the woods or a park. Determine now to conquer the battles that might try to prevent you from getting there.

Creative Punches

Retreating, of course, can have its challenges. Too often we feel if we set time aside for individual reflection, rest, and worship, we might be perceived as unproductive or irresponsible. So we put such times off or make excuses to avoid them. (Besides, unless your personality type is that of a severe introvert, being away from other people is tough.) Even if or when we do get to a place set apart and are just about ready to quiet our souls and minds, we can almost count on an interruption or something to distract us from our divine purpose. For instance, as I set out to write these chapters on solitude, I asked some friends who lived near the beach if I could stay and work in their home. While they were at work during the day, I would be surrounded by woods, quiet, and solitude. I would make morning bicycle trips to the beach, let the roar of the ocean and the splash of the salt water remind me of its Maker, so I could retreat to peaceful lonely afternoons of writing, void of the city noise I usually hear at my writing desk or the typical daily distractions of urban living.

Just as I was getting into this refreshing routine of solitary fellowship and working diligently away, the electrical power went out. Simply shut off. On the whole street. That meant no more computer—and no more writing—for me that afternoon. As I stared out at the sun playing through the trees, I could only imagine how the neighbors on both sides might be responding to the power shortage—they were each expecting dozens of guests in their homes that night. Hors d'oeuvres had to be made, vacuuming had to be done, punch bowls had to be filled. Now, there would be no electricity for their refrigerators, microwaves, or vacuums. Frantic chaos might very well be descending next door.

I, too, was faced with a choice: I could get angry and irritated that my plans for writing were interrupted, throw a little tantrum and kick the wall, or I could throw some creative punches and hang on to God's peaceful presence like Jacob did. Plan B seemed like the better option for my spiritual health (and my friend's home), so I pulled out a few books I needed to read and allowed myself to be redirected. I actually got so engrossed in the books that four hours later when the power came back on, I didn't even notice.

In his book *Out of Solitude*, the insightful Catholic theologian Henri J. Nouwen tells the story of a college professor who learned the art of letting go of his own agenda. "Looking back on his long life of teaching, the professor said with a funny wrinkle in his eyes: 'I have always been complaining that my work was constantly interrupted, until slowly I discovered that my interruptions were my work.' This is the great conversion in our life: to recognize and believe that many unexpected events are not just disturbing interruptions of our projects, but the way in which God molds our hearts and prepares us for his return."[1]

You see, when we have cultivated an attitude of solitary fellowship with the Almighty, when we are ever aware of his presence even in our interrupted, distracted lives, our sense of balance is solidified, our footing secured, and our hearts are at peace. This awareness sustains us and enables us then to do what God has given us to do. No matter where we go or what we are doing, whether we're in the quiet woods or on a crowded street, we can walk with certainty because our God is Emmanuel, God is with us. When God commanded Joshua to take charge of the Israelites, he promised, "The LORD your God will be with you wherever you go" (Josh. 1:9). When Christ commissioned his disciples to go and make disciples of all the nations, he promised, "Surely I will be with you always, to the very end of the age" (Matt. 28:20). And when the apostle John received the revelation of a time to come, there was no doubt in his mind who was standing with him. "'I am the Alpha and the Omega,' says the Lord God, 'who is, and who was, and who is to come, the Almighty'" (Rev. 1:8).

Make a list of metaphors of who God is: the Shepherd, Prince of Peace, Word made flesh, the River of Life, etc. Then remind yourself that it is this God in all his glory who walks with you daily.

Finding the Path

The apostle Paul wrote in Romans 8:31, "If God is for us, who can be against us?" With this as our foundation, we know that our solitary fellowship is established when we walk *with* him throughout each day; we don't just leave him in our living rooms or at the kitchen table when our "quiet times" are over in the morning. I have to admit that sometimes when I finish my dutiful reading and close my Bible in the mornings, I might as well say to God, "See you later. I've got things to do now." In other words, it's easy for me to forget the wonderful promise that God is with me as I enter the daily responsibilities he's placed before me. Rather than inviting him into them *with* me, I often allow them to distract me *from* him.

But if we know God will be with us and for us wherever we go and that there's no place we can be apart from him, how, then, do we cultivate a continual awareness of his presence, an active communicative exchange with him that lasts throughout the day, not just during our devotions? How do we learn to listen to him as much as we talk with him as we're driving to a meeting, riding the subway to work, helping a neighbor, or cooking dinner for our families?

Intentionally focusing our hearts and minds in solitude, that's how. And because we're all different, nurturing this

57

relationship will look different for each of us. One busy mother told me that she has her best talks with God in the shower, undistracted from her responsibilities with her family. That shower conversation sustains her through the rest of her full and important day. Another friend told me he has to go for a jog each morning to get things right with God; the physical exercise helps him clear his mind to hear from his Champion. And if she doesn't have her quiet moment in the corner of a local diner each morning, one woman told me she would be "lost and in a fog" throughout her busy day. "Believers find mines of silver and gold in solitary places; they fetch up precious jewels out of secret holes, out of the bottom of the ocean, where there are no inhabitants," said the sixteenth-century preacher George Swinnock.

The point is the anchor of solitary fellowship will take on different attributes according to our lifestyles and personalities. I was surprised and delighted recently when I picked up a mainstream women's magazine and read how one contemporary writer beautifully described such diversity:

> Solitude is a beautiful word. It sounds like sunlight through trees, or a walk on the beach, or a soprano voice that soars. Perhaps I hear the sound of "solace" in it, the replenishment that comes from finding what's at the center of self. It's a different word than "alone"; I hear a moan in alone, which turns so easily into "loneliness," and has more to do with a single tree on a prairie, or a child by herself on a crowded playground. Solitude is for those with an ample interior, with room to roam, well-provided with supplies. And I need a day or two, every so often, to make that journey.[2]

What a wonderful picture of what it means to go "roaming through our ample interior" with the Creator. Indeed, it is a unique experience for each of us because of our various backgrounds, cultural influences, and daily challenges. We should not assume that our Christian lives should be carbon copies or cookie cutter images of others just because we live in a nation in which 44 percent of its residents attend church regularly. That would seem contradictory to the creativity of our God and deny his incredible love for diversity. No, our unique individuality is a gift, and it will no doubt surface the more we are in touch with our Maker.

Solitary fellowship might best be nourished by walking on the beach where you feel his pleasure in the breaking waves, or letting the smile on a child's face remind you of God's delight in you, or taking a drive to the mountains to replenish your soul with the smell of pine, or enjoying a long hot shower in the morning to talk things over with your Father. The springboard into the company of Jesus will mean different things to each of us. There are, however, a number of intentional efforts—those "well-provided supplies"—we can all incorporate into our lives that can help us enjoy the feast of God's unchanging goodness.

Ask a close friend to reflect on what he or she sees as your unique characteristics. Then discuss how they might reflect the Creator.

Lessons in Quiet

One of the most effective ways to develop an awareness of the Incarnate God is to learn to embrace silence. For some people, silence immediately strikes terror in their hearts; it is so profoundly different from the background noise of the television or radio, the chatter of children, the clamor of cars and neighbors outside that the very thought

59

of entering it is like landing on an unexplored planet by yourself. Single friends who live alone have told me they can't stand to have their apartments quiet because it reminds them that they are alone. Quickly, they turn on the TV or the radio, not to watch or listen but just to hear the familiar noise of human voices.

But the reality is we are never really alone if we are *with* Christ. Perhaps silence is his tool for helping us confront the reality of ourselves, our painful struggles, and our need for God in both. Because silence makes us more aware of who we are and who we aren't, more aware of the life and hurts within us and around us, it is a territory some of us would rather deny than encounter. So we avoid this strange friend called silence and pretend it doesn't exist by going to the movies, watching television, running from meetings to lunch appointments to Bible studies. We switch on our radios or Christian tapes when we get home, and we call friends on the telephone to remind us of anything but what we know silence will tell us: We are depraved and needy.

In her book *Meeting God in Silence*, Sara Park McLaughlin addresses this very issue: "Silence is more than a temporary lull in racket. It is an awesome, sobering condition, an experience that brings us face to face with ourselves and with God."[3] Yes, silence is a sobering confrontation with honesty about ourselves, and to those who know no hope or grace, of course, that is a dreadful thing. Who wants to remember how inept or insecure or hurting we are? But for those of us who understand we are sinful beings but that the mercies of God and his commitment to changing us for his sake are greater than we could ever imagine, silence and the fruit it produces can be a liberating and exhilarating experience.

I learned firsthand the power of silence when one semester I gave my college students an interesting assignment in our communication class. We were at a Christian college so I knew that many of my students had some understanding of a relationship with the Triune God. Many were from fine Christian homes and had attended nice Christian high schools before coming to our university. But when I gave them this particular assignment, many reacted in, shall we say, rather un-Christian manners.

I was requiring that they go on what we would call a "media fast" for one entire week. Their eyes got big as I explained that for seven whole days they could watch no television, see no videos or films, listen to no radio or tapes, and read no newspapers or magazines. If they were worried they wouldn't know what was going on in the world, they could ask friends or family members for such information. I encouraged them to spend time in silence, to take walks or drives alone, to write in their journals, or to pick up the Bible or other books for reflection. I even suggested they consider using the time they would ordinarily use to watch their favorite sitcom to study for their courses. (That was a novel idea for some.) And if they had to have human contact, they could call a friend or meet at a coffee shop. At the end of the week, they were to write about how the experience affected them and give a short presentation to the class as well.

Most of the thirty or so students would rather have had me assign them twenty one-hundred-page research papers than a week without the media! Immediately, I was met with great resistance: "Our favorite football team is playing this week!" "I can't do anything without my music on!" "I have a date; what are we supposed to do now if we can't go to a movie?" They yelled and hollered and threw the best college temper tantrums I have seen in eighteen years of teaching before or since. But they did it. Some of them did, anyway. A few students flat out refused to participate in the fast.

One week later I listened with great interest to their results. One student found she could not remember a week of her life when she had been more productive: She had written long-overdue letters, finished class assignments, and felt closer to God than she had in years. Another told us he had been really wary of the assignment but had discovered more creative ways to be with people than "always going to movies and concerts." Perhaps the most moving story came from a twenty-year-old woman who had had a terrible fight with her best friend the week before the media fast was to begin. She had decided to drive to her friend's house to end the friendship. En route, her radio blared heavy metal songs as she grew angrier and more bitter. She replayed in her mind the mean-spirited exchange she had had and planned the speech she was going to give her now-former friend. Halfway to the house, she suddenly remembered the assignment, turned off the music, and tuned into the silence. To her surprise, her anger began to subside, and she remembered to pray. By the time she arrived at her friend's home, she had decided to ask for forgiveness from her friend, and they reconciled the relationship.

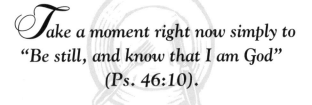

Take a moment right now simply to "Be still, and know that I am God" (Ps. 46:10).

Festive Souls

In silence, our hearts and minds are quieted enough for God's Spirit to direct us into truth and healing. The dross of our sinful souls rises in the process and escapes from our lips in a freeing form of confession. "Here in the presence of Almighty God, I kneel in silence, and with penitent and obedient heart confess my sins, so that I may obtain forgiveness by your infinite goodness and mercy. Amen," so says the Book of Common Prayer. And so true indeed.

As our inner spirits are quieted before the Eternal Judge, we recognize our sins, bring them into his hands and watch, amazed and grateful, as he throws them into the sea. It is a purifying exchange, for as George Macdonald said, "To be humbly ashamed is to be plunged in the cleansing bath of truth."

One of Macdonald's greatest fans understood such a reality. In C. S. Lewis's conversion account, he continues his story of confession:

> Really, a young Atheist cannot guard his faith too carefully. Dangers lie in wait for him on every side. You must not do, you must not even try to do, the will of the Father unless you are prepared to "know of the doctrine." All my acts, desires, and thoughts were to be brought into harmony with universal Spirit. For the first time I examined myself with a seriously practical purpose. And there I found what appalled me; a zoo of lusts, a bedlam of ambitions, a nursery of fears, a harem of fondled hatreds. My name was legion.[4]

As silence drives us into recognition of our "legion," confession to the Father lunges it out. And from such confession emerges a joyful celebration of the new life Christ has given us with him. We cannot help but worship him, dancing and singing in our souls, over the burdens we let go of through silence and confession. We turn to the Prophets, the Psalms, the Gospels, the Letters of the Apostles, and we see with new eyes how God's redemptive hand has again changed what was once intended for evil into the good of his purposes. We retreat to a center or a corner of the world, we journal, we protect our time with him because we know when we reenter the daily endeavors he has placed before us that we will be stronger, more graceful, more in tune with the rhythm of his life because we are holding tight to the hand of the one in charge.

It is indeed as Mother Teresa described in the following: "We need to find God and he cannot be found in noise and restlessness. . . . See how nature—trees, flowers, grass—grow in silence; see the stars, the moon, the sun, how they move in silence. . . . The more we receive in silent prayer, the more we can give in our active life. We need silence to be able to touch souls."[5]

Christ himself knew unless he "withdrew to lonely places and prayed," as Luke 5:16 tells us, his ministry of truth and care for a people void of both would have been much more draining. When we see him "relaxing" at Martha and Mary's home, he encourages Martha to enjoy the time with him, rather than the busyness around her. And when we watch him in Gethsemane, deeply distressed at what was to come, we see him hanging on to his time alone with God.

Yes, our solitude with God is his practical way of imparting his presence and characteristics to us. *With* him, we are prepared to serve. And our attitude toward service—the second spiritual food group—is directly proportional to our solitary fellowship.

Be a Mary and sit for a few minutes at Jesus' feet!

4

SERVICE:
CHOPPING THOSE ONIONS

When you cease to make a contribution, you begin to die.
ELEANOR ROOSEVELT

I was twenty-two years old before I ever knew what it meant to serve. Growing up in a suburban middle-class community instilled in me a keen aptitude for self-centered independence, and I became a master at thinking only of myself, getting what I wanted, when I wanted it. In fact, the only time I heard the word *serve* was on the tennis court! My family was often too busy with our own separate lives to care about anyone else's, and even after I became a Christian through a local youth organization, my world continued to revolve around me and me alone. By college, I continued to seek opportunities that I thought would benefit me, considering very little how my decisions might affect others. In fact, in my self-focused perspective, Jesus existed to help me with my problems, guide me through them, and encourage me to keep going. Period.

So when I saw Rick and Joyce Cole actually looking for opportunities to serve other people, I was stunned. Here was a middle-aged Christian couple showing me for the first time in my life what it meant to live out an attitude of service, to reflect their love for Christ in their actions. The Coles had been friends of my oldest brother, active leaders in a variety of youth ministries and community organizations, and willing to help out recent college graduates—like me—who were wondering how to enter life's next transition called adulthood. When I moved into a neighborhood near them to begin my teaching career, I often found myself on their doorstep. I was drawn to their humility, attracted to their lifestyle of giving.

The Coles didn't own much. They lived in a mobile home. Rick worked at a printing shop while taking a few college courses at night to complete his bachelor's degree, and Joyce taught dance classes and sponsored the cheerleaders at a nearby high school for extra income. They were talented musicians and performed often at youth concerts, churches, and coffeehouses.

But it wasn't their talents or career choices that first drew me to them. I saw in them a quality I had always yearned for: genuine concern for others. Rick was always meeting someone for coffee, giving people a ride somewhere in his beat-up blue car, or helping out a friend with home projects. Joyce was always baking cookies for her high school students, sewing outfits for somebody's newborn baby, or preparing special dinners for sick neighbors. This couple lived out their Christian faith by actually getting involved in people's lives, serving them, and caring for their needs.

And that had a tremendous impact on me. For the next few years, I watched Rick and Joyce as together they served in their community, their church, and throughout the city. They lived simply so they could give much. They prayed fervently so they could act wisely. They were servants of Christ, the greatest Servant, because they shared the same attitude he possessed, an attitude that manifested itself in their lives in countless ways and affected more people than just this selfish, young Christian woman. For the first time in my life, I began to recognize that to be a balanced follower of Christ, I needed to learn the secret of service.

Consider someone in your life whose active faith has helped you understand more about Christ. Ask God to refresh them now in their giving. You might consider dropping them a note of encouragement for their example.

Selfish Distractions

The problem I've had with my self-centered Christianity is one I've noticed most North American Christians struggle with: Instead of coming to God because of who he is, we come for what we can get. Perhaps our instant-gratification society has taught us that our wants and needs can be met on demand, and therefore, we think a relationship

67

with Christ will do the same. We give God our wish list and expect full compliance, relegating him to the position of Cosmic Caretaker, a spiritual genie who responds to our desires and longings when we snap our fingers because that is what he's for. After all, if we are his children, why wouldn't he want to give us everything we ask for?

No wonder service becomes a difficult concept to embrace for many Western evangelicals; we're so busy expecting God to be our servant, running our own lives with self on the throne, that serving others is nothing more than an inconvenience or a distraction from our devotion to ourselves. I'm embarrassed to admit that for a long time I actually dreaded the idea of going to a friend's house for dinner. What if I would be asked to help prepare something or do the dishes afterward? Honestly, I viewed service as a lot of trouble, a bother that required me to muster up all the energy I could just to wash a few plates or chop an onion. I was so centered on my self that it was difficult to consider the needs of others.

I think many of us respond to service in the same way I reacted to chopping onions for dinner: We know we should do it, but we really don't like the stink or the pain it brings to our eyes. There's nothing glamorous about onions—they're never a main course or a crucial ingredient in a dish. No one really notices the contribution anyway, so why bother? Besides, there's nothing in it for us, right?

So what good could it possibly do to serve others? What difference would it make? And how does serving others help provide balance in our lives? Certainly, if we're honest, we've all wondered about these questions at one time or another. In fact, one of literature's most famous characters considers these very issues, yet concludes that nothing on earth could be more important than making money for himself. That is, until a horrifying encounter with a world of ghosts transforms him into thinking otherwise.

We all know the story: In Charles Dickens's *A Christmas Carol*, the selfish curmudgeon known as Ebenezer Scrooge is finally forced to face reality. Ebenezer hasn't got a kind bone in his body; everything he does is full of bitterness and selfishness. On Christmas Eve, though, his old business partner, Jacob Marley, pays a visit to reprimand the old miser. There's only one small problem, however, with such a visit: Jacob died several years earlier! Still, the dead partner comes to confront Scrooge's stingy ways, mocking his self-centered life, and then warning him of what could happen if he doesn't begin to think of others, including the terrible visitations Scrooge will receive later that night. Jacob's message is strong, urging his living partner to move beyond self-absorption and into a lifestyle that daily considers his fellow man. The ghost is bound by chains and misery, which have become his eternal lot for ignoring service to others, and our protagonist is terrified at the prospect of what could happen to him as well:

> Scrooge fell upon his knees, and clasped his hands before his face.
> "Mercy!" he said. "Dreadful apparition, why do you trouble me?"
> "Man of the worldly mind!" replied the Ghost. "Do you believe in me or not?"
> "I do," said Scrooge, trembling. . . . "You are fettered. Tell me why?"
> "I wear the chain I forged in life," replied the Ghost. "I made it link by link, and yard by yard; I girded it on my own free will, and of my own free will I wore it. . . . Oh! Captive, bound and double-ironed," cried the phantom, "Not to know that any Christian spirit working kindly in its little sphere, whatever it may be, will find its mortal life too short for its vast means of usefulness! Not to know that no space of regret can make amends for one life's opportunities misused! Yet such was I! Oh, such was I!"

69

"But you were always a good man of business, Jacob," faltered Scrooge, who now began to apply this to himself.

"Business!" cried the Ghost, wringing its hands again. "Mankind was my business. The common welfare was my business; charity, mercy, forbearance, and benevolence were, all, my business. The dealings of my trade were but a drop of water in the comprehensive ocean of my business!"

It held up its chain at arm's length, as if that were the cause of all its unavailing grief, and flung it heavily upon the ground again.

"At this time of the rolling year," the specter said, "I suffer most. Why did I walk through crowds of fellow beings with my eyes turned down, and never raise them to that blessed Star which led the Wise Men to a poor abode? Were there no poor homes to which its light would have conducted me?"

Scrooge was very much dismayed to hear the specter going on at this rate and began to quake exceedingly.[1]

Marley's confession that he ignored the true "business of mankind," that is, of caring for those in need, is a powerful charge to consider forsaking selfish ways for the sake of others. He deeply regrets not looking into the eyes of the poor as he passed them on the streets, or leading them to the "blessed Star." The words weigh heavy on the frightened old man, and consequently, Scrooge's "quaking" turns into one of the most moving conversions in literary history: He wakes the next morning (after an interesting night, to say the least) a new man, overjoyed with the idea of service, intent on meeting the needs of his "fellow beings" and making "mankind his business" from this time forward. He is ecstatic in his giving, delighted over his change of heart. And very much alive. Every December when I see such a transformation either on the stage of a local theater production or as a friend reads the story aloud, I am struck by what happens when sinful humans encounter the joy of service.

What specific things might keep you from caring for others?

Scrooge's initial "anti-service" attitude developed because he couldn't see the value in such deeds, especially since they only distracted him from his own endeavors. Obviously, this attitude displays a faulty understanding of what service really is. Authentic Christian service is never so burdensome that we have to force ourselves to perform some praiseworthy act of charity because we think it is our duty. Sinful human nature (as Scrooge shows us) does not naturally look out for the best interest of others, though we often live under the heavy weight of "shoulds" and obligations. (And some of us might have a greater propensity to serve because of our personality types or upbringings.) We think we *should* wash the dishes after a meal because that is polite. Or we *should* sponsor a child in a poor country because that's a good thing to do. When we do, even these acts can be self-serving because they are often motivated by what *we* think will improve our status, or appease our conscience. Yet, these, in fact, are what the prophet Isaiah referred to as he recognized the futility of our human efforts: "All of us have become like one who is unclean, and all our righteous acts are like filthy rags; we all shrivel up like a leaf, and like the wind our sins sweep us away" (64:6).

To God, the Maker of the universe who does not really need our help or assistance, even our most valiant acts of charity are like "filthy rags." Why? Because he is not so concerned with what we do as with who we are. And who we are as Christians always leads us back to him. Yes, the paradox of creation is that we are all sinful, needy beings

71

who care little for the "business of mankind." But we are also made in God's image, an image that inherently gives and provides and assists, one full of "charity, mercy, forbearance, and benevolence." So it is only when we come into his presence in solitude, nurturing a solitary fellowship with God, confronting our selfishness and cultivating a solid interior filled *by* him in continual communion *with him,* that we understand the true nature of service. Before we can ever go out into the world to serve, we must first come into the presence of the one who is, thankfully, also in the business of changing us from self-centered individuals to service-oriented vessels for *his* sake. Scrooge-like conversions are still possible!

In other words, I like to say that service is "an outflow of the inflow." We mustn't view service as another task in our already busy spiritual careers, otherwise God merely acts as our boss. Rather, from a consistent intake of solitude comes an attitude of service, one very different from the obligatory duty of religious or humanitarian acts. Time spent honestly with Christ changes us from demanding, spoiled children to liberated reflections of his giving nature. Here in solitary fellowship, even the most selfish soul can be transformed into one that looks for opportunities to demonstrate the compassion and grace of God. We want to love others because he does. We want to care for their needs because he does. As Oswald Chambers wrote, "Our service is to be a living sacrifice of devotion to Jesus, the secret of which is identity *with* Him in suffering, in death, and in resurrection" (emphasis mine). All acts of true service, then, come first from reception of his love and next from a sincere desire to please God as our friend, our first love, and our Lord. This very attitude, or as Webster defines attitude, this "posture, manner or disposition" is developed in direct proportion to the amount of solitary fellowship we experience in our lives.

Giving Back

We know, then, that Christ himself is our example, indeed the very personification of service, and consequently, the cornerstone for a balanced life. After discussing the importance of being focused on others, the apostle Paul reminded the Christians at Philippi of the Lord's disposition for service: "Your attitude should be the same as that of Christ Jesus: Who, being in very nature God, did not consider equality with God something to be grasped, but made himself nothing, taking the very nature of a servant, being made in human likeness. And being found in appearance as a man, he humbled himself and became obedient to death—even death on a cross!" (Phil. 2:5–8). Christ's whole being was to serve; all that he did, prayed, and said was so that others could live abundantly. From his birth, through his life and death, and even after his resurrection, we watch a man who is completely empty of human self, yet completely full of divine service.

What do you think of when you hear the word service?

But what does it mean to serve? The dictionary defines it as to "attend or wait upon; work for; aid; be a substitute for; avail." If we are to have an attitude or disposition of service, one that mirrors Christ's, then we will be (supernaturally) attending to the needs of others, working to bring comfort, and at times, actually becoming "a substitute for" or "taking on the very nature of" someone in pain.

73

During my second year of teaching (and watching the Coles), a student of mine was tragically murdered by her estranged father. I was numb as I heard the horrible story. When I called Joyce on the phone with the news, the first and only thing she said to me was, "I'll be right over." For the next few hours, she "availed" herself by actually sharing the loss of this young person with me in my apartment. Her presence was a human "substitute" of God's comfort. "Jesus with skin on," as one pastor would call it.

There is no greater privilege as Christians than to encounter Christ in the act of service. It requires that we move beyond ourselves in caring for the needs of others, regardless of the cost. If service is the "act or result of serving; duty performed or needs supplied; religious worship," then obviously, service assumes that there is a need and a way to meet that need, however great or small, often drawing both parties into the replenishing waters of worshiping the Creator. This attitude of service, which springs from our solitary fellowship with Jehovah Jireh, the great Provider, satisfies and benefits others, but it also changes us. In other words, true service always means there is mutuality involved. It is not simply a onetime effort, like giving old clothes to the homeless at Christmas time, or showing up once a year to volunteer at a program. Christian service is never "once in a while," nor is it patronizing or self-seeking. Instead, it flows out of a genuine concern for the long-term well-being of another. It responds spontaneously as well as thoughtfully, proactively as well as reactively.

That's why receiving is as much a part of an attitude of service as giving. Many of us, especially those who have chosen service-oriented careers such as social work, nursing, or ministry, would often rather give than receive. We find it easier to extend help or assistance than to receive it ourselves. Perhaps pride or a need for control moves us to keep service one-sided. But when we allow others to give back to us, we affirm their dignity as humans; we communicate to them that we value their contribution. We validate their significance as creations made in the image of God because they are reflecting his very nature by giving.

Christ displayed this type of mutuality in the beautiful story of Luke 7:36–50. One of the religious leaders had invited Jesus to dinner at his home, and chances are, the place was filled with wealthy guests, a variety of exquisite foods, and many interesting conversations. Somehow, a woman "who had lived a sinful life" found out about the party and decided to crash it. She had heard of this Jesus, this man who served and welcomed outcasts, forgave sins, and offered new chances to people like her. She slipped by the doorman and wandered into the chatting room without much notice. And as soon as she saw the Savior, something happened inside her. She began to weep, broken by the hope of change that full acceptance always brings. Then with her tears, she began to wipe his feet—dry, dusty feet that had walked miles throughout the hot desertlike region. Never mind what people might have been thinking about this woman; she was completely uninhibited in her willingness to serve the great Servant. Nothing could hold her back.

Then she broke an alabaster jar of perfume over his feet, an extremely expensive jar that no doubt had cost all she had earned from her "nighttime career." Her shoulders shook from the weeping, yet she could not help but lean over these tired toes, kissing them, wiping them with her long dark hair, and then pouring the sweet smelling liquid to soothe them. Not once did Jesus interrupt her or resist her. Not once did he say, "Oh, no, that's okay. Let me serve *you* instead. You need more help than *I* do." No, he understood the dignity and healing that came with letting this woman serve him. He knew how important it was for her to give back to him. He allowed her to "love much" because she had been forgiven much.

The Pharisee hosting the party was not happy. The woman's act of abandon, her humble gift of service, had embarrassed him in front of some of the most prominent people in town. He himself was humbled and admonished by both the woman's act and the words of his honored guest. And sometimes, indeed, that's what happens when we see others giving out of their incredible pain and difficult circumstances—our spirits are gently scolded, challenged to consider the motives and attitudes of our own hearts. Allowing others to give back is an exchange that must be allowed, an element of authentic service that must not be forgotten or ignored.

Of course, I am not saying that we serve so we will get something in return; that's manipulation. Unfortunately, modern-day charity is often manipulative, guilt-induced, impersonal, and one-sided. We write a check to the Salvation Army or the mercy ministry of our church, drop off used toys at the children's hospital or the urban center because these things are easier than looking into someone's eyes and offering them a friendship instead. And though onetime charity can be helpful or could be considered a tithe, it must not be confused with an authentic attitude of Christlike service.

Instead, when Christians actually identify with the pain or needs of another, we are most reflecting the Light of the World. Identification goes beyond charity and reflects a heart that is humble, mutually respectful, and relational. It seeks to bear the burdens of hurting people throughout the process of their healing journey. It is coming alongside the outcast as an equal, not an authority, living as a neighbor in places of poverty, or becoming "Jesus" to the troubled or downcast soul. We identify with the hurt or situation of others as together we seek to meet the need or solve the problem. Since Christ "became flesh and made his dwelling among us" (John 1:14) as the incarnation, so, too, must we lovingly identify with others in their suffering and encourage them in their own service.

Identification assumes equality because the concerns of others become our concerns. It is "our" problem, not "theirs." Charity, on the other hand, does not invite relationship and can be divisive: One who has gives to the one who has not, and ends it there. Identification, rather, says all have sinned, all are in need of a Savior and the mutual help of a friend. As one Christian counselor put it, we are all simply "wounded healers," one begger telling another where to find food. Therefore, reciprocal joy and love quite naturally come from an attitude of pure service, nurtured by solitary fellowship with the Father. Christ's ultimate example of serving through his sacrifice on the cross confirms this and always calls us back into relationship with him.

Recall a time when you needed to receive help or the service of another. How did it affect you?

Unique Service

The beautiful thing about serving as a Christian is that it happens *after* we've met with the one who gave himself in the ultimate act of service; we don't have to serve to get to him. This unique quality of service in the Christian faith is astonishingly different from other world religions. Many other belief systems, for instance, suggest that good works or proper, moral deeds can provide the path to salvation, perfection, or heaven. The emphasis in these others is on the individual's efforts to live a good life in order to atone for his sin or bad life; for the Christian believer, however, Christ has done the work already on the cross and gives us his grace, character, and Holy Spirit to live a life "worthy of the calling" (Eph. 4:1). We do nothing but open our hands to receive his compassion, which then spills out of our hands into gracious acts of mutual service.

Other faiths suggest that a person's good deeds, his human efforts, alone will make him worthy of his spiritual goal. For instance, Hindus and Buddhists alike place an important emphasis on karma, defined in Webster's as "the ethical consequences of the totality of one's actions that determine the destiny of one's subsequent existence (or existences) until one has achieved spiritual liberation." Hindus believe that if an individual experiences bad karma, it's because he did something terribly bad in a past life. However, if a person has good karma, it means he has done good deeds in the past. Hindus also believe humans are trapped in samsara, which is a meaningless cycle of birth, life, death, and rebirth. Since karma is the accumulated sum of one's good and bad deeds and determines how an individual will live his next life, moral acts, thoughts, and devotion can help one be reborn at a higher level. Eventually, one can even escape samsara to achieve enlightenment. Bad deeds, on the other hand, can cause a person to be reborn at a lower level, or even as an animal. The unequal distribution of wealth, prestige, and suffering are seen as natural consequences for previous acts in former lives.

Buddhists, too, believe their good lives will ultimately lead them to nirvana ("a state of detachment and dispassion"). For example, they do not believe in a transcendent God or gods, the need for a personal savior, the power of prayer, or eternal life in a heaven or hell after death on earth. They do believe in reincarnation, or the concept that one must go through many cycles of birth, living, and death. After many such cycles, if a person releases his attachment to desire and to self, he can attain nirvana. The way to get there is to follow Buddha's Eightfold Path, which consists of: (1) right understanding; (2) right thinking; (3) right speech; (4) right conduct; (5) right livelihood; (6) right effort; (7) right mindfulness; and (8) right concentration. If you are able to discipline yourself enough in these eight areas of "right" living, you are nirvana-bound.

Baha'i religion also perceives service as a major cornerstone for an individual's personal liberation. Some of Bahaullah's most famous sayings are, "The best beloved of all things in My sight is justice," "The earth is but one country, and mankind its citizens," and "The well-being of mankind, its peace and security, are unattainable unless and until its unity is firmly established." Unlike most religions that attempt to preserve the past, Baha'i beliefs promote major social changes that originated in the nineteenth century: They support gender and race equality, world government, freedom of expression and assembly, and world peace. To Hare Krishnas, hell is a temporary destination after death for people who have sinned greatly while on earth. Devotees need a spiritual master, and even have what they call "Nine Processes of Devotional Service." To Muslims, an intensely moral life and strict devotion to Allah will put a person in good standing on judgment day. And in traditional Jewish beliefs, believers respond to God's deliverance by fulfilling mitzvoth, or divine commandments, all 613 of them.

Certainly, each religion's devotion to service, morality, and justice can be good things for producing personal betterment and world progress. Those who espouse such beliefs are to be respected and treated with kindness and grace, not judgment. But the pressure for any human to have to earn his way to God, heaven, or perfection by his own good works of service creates a sad and difficult life of compro-

79

mise and deception. In these other religions, good works or acts of service are required if a person is to obtain salvation or closeness to the Creator. Christianity, however, reveals to us our own sinfulness and need for a Savior to invite us out of sin and into right relationship with God. *He* then serves the world through our personal relationship with him. Christ the Person is already our salvation, and nothing we can or cannot do can earn his favor. Service for the Christian, then, is merely reflecting the image of the greatest Servant who ever lived; it comes as a natural outflow from our relationship with him, not as a means of getting to him. In other words, we don't serve to get *to* God; we serve because we've been *with* God.

The Family Resemblance

The more we consider and know about the life of Christ during his time on earth, the more we will see his amazing distinction from any other "prophet" and the more his likeness will be seen in us. Just as compassion, grace, justice, caring, and provision are characteristics of our heavenly Father, so, too, should they be characteristics of his children. When people look at us, then, they should see the mark of Christ in our lives, they should notice the "family resemblance" as we help others. Because we serve—giving to and receiving from—those in need, we look most like Christ.

Consider how people responded to Christ as he walked through Jerusalem and Samaria. Many could not stay away from him, so drawn were they to his loving nature that they gave up all they had to follow him. But others (namely those in authority) were so indignant toward him that they planned his demise. Either way, for or against, people noticed this humble carpenter who was changing the world with his lifestyle of service. They still do.

Sometimes I wonder if the Scribes and Pharisees weren't more bothered by the lifestyle of Jesus than by his radical teaching; they saw him serving the poor and feeding the hungry, heard of him healing the brokenhearted, witnessed him affirming the social outcast. Try as they may, they just could not keep him from reaching out to people in need, from affirming them, loving them, and inviting them into a life-changing relationship with God.

His marvelous proclamation of service quoted from the Book of Isaiah, the first words Jesus spoke in public *after* (of course) his forty days of fasting and solitude in the wilderness, only made matters worse for the skeptics: "The Spirit of the Lord is on me, because he has anointed me to preach good news to the poor. He has sent me to proclaim freedom for the prisoners and recovery of sight for the blind, to release the oppressed, to proclaim the year of the Lord's favor" (Luke 4:18–19).

An attitude of service permeated Christ's entire life, spilling over into his relationships, his words, his decisions, his emotions. Why did he weep over Jerusalem? Or cry for the death of his friend Lazarus? Because his heart was broken for others. Why did he allow Mary to wash his feet with her hair? Because he discerned what was best for her and loved her enough to let her give to him. Why did he go through Samaria and ask a woman of disrepute to draw water from the well for him? Because he wanted to affirm the social outcast, a "minority" woman who had not known grace or love or dignity in her society. And why did Jesus touch a leper, heal the blind man, provide bread for the masses, go to the cross, and shatter the tomb? Because he could not contain his love for others; his entire being wanted to bring healing and wholeness so others might know his Father in an intimate, life-giving relationship.

Even the night before his death, knowing he would die a horrendous death and then be separated from his

81

heavenly Father for three days, Jesus still sought to serve by washing his disciples' feet. Service defined Christ's purpose on earth, and it should define ours as well. Our responsibility and privilege as children of God is not to be a servant *of* Christ but a servant *with* Christ. Why? Because service distinguished his entire being and marked his ministry from start to finish more than any other religious figure in all of history. In fact, Christ could not *not* serve.

One of the best books I've read on Christ's character of compassionate service is Henri J. Nouwen's *Compassion: A Reflection on the Christian Life*. In it, he describes Christ's attitude of identification and service expressed in a variety of actions:

> When Jesus saw the crowd harassed and dejected like sheep without a shepherd, he felt with them in the center of his being (Matthew 9:36). When he saw the blind, the paralyzed, and the deaf being brought to him from all directions, he trembled from within and experienced their pains in his own heart (Matthew 14:14). When he noticed that the thousands who had followed him for days were tired and hungry, he said, I am moved with compassion (Mark 8:2). . . . They moved him, they made him feel with all his intimate sensibilities the depth of their sorrow. He became lost with the lost, hungry with the hungry, and sick with the sick. In him, all suffering was sensed with a perfect sensitivity. The great mystery revealed to us in this is that Jesus, who is the sinless son of God, chose in total freedom to suffer fully our pains and thus to let us discover the true nature of our own passions. In him, we see and experience the persons we truly are. He who is divine lives our broken humanity not as a curse but as a blessing. His divine compassion makes it possible for us to face our sinful selves, because it transforms our broken human condition from a cause of despair into a source of hope.[2]

And so when we serve *with* this Christ of compassion, this man who took on more than we could ever endure to give us more than we could ever expect, we come face to face with the joy of service.

Spend a few minutes reflecting on the life of Christ on earth. Imagine him walking, touching, crying, praying with his friends.

5

SERVICE:
WORKING IN THE KITCHEN

*If only I could so live and so serve the world that after me
there should never again be birds in cages.*

ISAK DINESEN

She was an unwed mother, abandoned by the baby's father
and left without much money to care for her child. It was the
late 1920s and the city in which she lived, New York, was
not very kind to young single mothers, especially if they wandered in and out of newspaper offices and publishing houses
looking for writing jobs. (Hardly the work of young mothers

in the twenties!) It didn't help that she had several communist friends and other "strange" associates. The young woman
was treated with suspicion and mistrust every time she turned
the corner; what possible use, people wondered, could she
have for the small Catholic parishes she was starting to visit?

When the stock market crashed in 1929 and sent the
entire country into an economic depression, the determined
young journalist with the piercing gaze and square jaw rolled
up her sleeves to help. She remembered how much the
Catholic sisters had helped when her baby came and her
lover left, providing fresh bread, diaper cloths, and spiritual
support. Their faith in action had intrigued her, and before
long she had become a regular attender at mass, kneeling,
praying, and worshiping alongside working-class families,
nuns, and vagrants. No, her communist friends were not at
all happy about her conversion, but the young woman could
not help but respond to this love that had met her in her
crisis. Now she would show the world her newfound Christian faith by serving others in *their* poverty and need.

And that's just what she did. Dorothy Day spent the next
fifty years of her life living among homeless men and women
(whom she called "our guests") and caring for the poor
through the Catholic Worker soup kitchens she founded.
Her legacy of service to those on the fringe of society can
be seen today in countless Catholic Worker homes, communities, and kitchens in cities across the country. If ever
there was an example in this century of Christian service,
of faith in action, it can be found in Dorothy Day. She never
stopped using her gift of writing, never stopped fighting for
justice, never stopped caring for the poor. Why? Because of
her relationship with God, an attitude of service was birthed
in her heart and nurtured in her lifestyle.

Just as service kept Dorothy Day from a life of self-pity
and despair during a personally difficult time, so, too, does
service help us keep our spiritual balance by causing us to
look upward and then outward. When we look out of our-

selves to care for the needs of others, when we share with others the love we've received from God, we stand firmly in the place we've been called to, our feet planted in the anchor of hope we've discovered in Christ, the Servant King. When God's character is born in our hearts, it becomes an attitude of service that quite naturally seeks an outward act to express it. Of course, we don't all have to live among the urban poor like Dorothy did to demonstrate our Christian faith. But we can open a door for a stranger, offer a smile and a welcome to a new neighbor, visit an elderly friend in a nursing home—you name it. There are hundreds of creative ways we can serve anywhere we are. And when we do, the world begins to recognize that there is some greater force at work than mere human concern.

A New Norm

Once when Christ was speaking with his disciples, a well-meaning mother approached him. She was concerned for her sons' futures and hoped that by networking with this up-and-coming young carpenter-leader, they would be set for life. "Grant that one of these two sons of mine may sit at your right and the other at your left in your kingdom," she asked the thirty-something Jewish leader (Matt. 20:21). No bones about it—she knew that to get ahead in this world, her boys had to capitalize on their contacts and make the most of their opportunities. This guy Jesus was going to be a mover and a shaker, she could tell.

When the others heard her request, they became indignant, not because of the selfish absurdity of it but because they, too, wanted such status and power. Jesus, however, saw through them all. He must have smiled as he called them together and shook his head as he corrected them. Gently, he then gave them the real definition of success: "Whoever

87

wants to become great among you must be your servant, and whoever wants to be first must be your slave—just as the Son of Man did not come to be served, but to serve, and to give his life as a ransom for many" (Matt. 20:26–28).

Our ultimate example of how to live our lives is found in the one who came not to be served but to serve. For the Christian, then, the wonderful thing about service is that our only qualification is willingness, and our greatest reward is God's pleasure (which, of course, spills over into our hearts!). We are not *driven* by it, we are *called* to it, revealing the gracious relationship between the Son of man and the one who has been ransomed by him. As we all know, service will probably never make us famous, rich, or powerful, that is, in the worldly sense, though it will in God's eyes. Though the world might never honor a servant's efforts, it will almost always respect it, if even anonymously.

There is also a lovely obscurity to service, just as preparations in the kitchen hours before a meal can create a joyful attitude of secret satisfaction. Often, no one sees the effort and hard work you've put into cutting the carrots, whipping the butter, or basting the bird. After they taste the fruit of your labor, they still might not know how much you sacrificed to make their bellies and palates happy. But you don't care; it was the sheer joy of the act itself that motivated you, not the response you might receive. That's because true service will not seek recognition from those at the table, only from the one who's preparing an eternal banquet for us. And as we live simply as Christ-bearers, our faith in action, our creative "kitchen work," will naturally reflect the ultimate Servant in a tangible, reciprocal, and often delicious form to those who are hungry and hurting.

Service, then, is every Christian's privilege and joy. Yet, sometimes it requires a price or a sacrifice, as it did our Lord. Shortly before his terrible death in 1968, the Rev. Dr. Martin Luther King Jr. spoke from the pulpit of Ebenezer Baptist Church on the true greatness of Christian service for anybody who is willing to follow Christ into the world.

(This sermon entitled "The Drum Major Instinct" was later played at his funeral.)

> Jesus gave us a new norm of greatness. If you want to be important—wonderful. If you want to be recognized—wonderful. If you want to be great—wonderful. But recognize that he who is greatest among you shall be your servant. That's your new definition of greatness, it means that everybody can be great. Because everybody can serve. You don't have to have a college degree to serve. You don't have to make your subject and your verb agree to serve. You don't have to know about Plato and Aristotle to serve. You don't have to know Einstein's theory of relativity to serve. You don't have to know the second theory of thermodynamics in physics to serve. You only need a heart full of grace. A soul generated by love. And you can be that servant.[1]

Everyone can experience the joy and mystery of Christlike service because, as Dr. King put it, everyone qualifies. The only thing required of the Christian who serves is a "heart full of grace, a soul generated by love." Neither comes necessarily from seminary or Sunday school class, but rather from a consistent exchange with the master of greatness, the one who showed us how to serve by giving his life on the cross. If our faith in Christ is alive and active, we will show it by our deeds as we seek to meet the needs of those around us.

Read James 2:14–22.
How are faith and deeds linked together?

When God begins to teach us about this "new norm" Jesus set regarding service, we will be challenged to get outside of our own pains and problems enough to concentrate on helping others. But that's not easy. Often, we are too centered on our own lives, relationships, or careers to care for others. Besides, we can be easily overwhelmed at the needs we see regularly in our neighborhoods or in the media. Where do we begin when the statistics are so discouraging? Over thirty-six million people living in the United States live in poverty and probably will never read this book. Nearly 20 percent of American children grow up in low-income families (i.e., families with incomes below the poverty level), one in ten Americans receives food stamps, and one out of every four kids in the United States lives in what most of us would call third-world poverty. This is double the child poverty rate of any other industrialized country. The number of homeless families has increased significantly in the past decade; families with children are currently the fastest growing group of the homeless population, approximately 40 percent. Thirty-five percent of homeless women and children are fleeing abuse, 25 percent of the single adult homeless population suffers from some form of manageable mental illness, and 22 percent of the general homeless population likely suffer from a substance abuse disorder.

It's obvious that the pain and needs of others (especially those in poverty) is a real, even ironic, issue for those of us living in the wealthiest nation on earth. When we consider, too, how welfare benefits make up only 1 percent of the federal budget, we wonder why so many politicians and religious leaders continually blame the poor for our national budget crisis. Certainly, the needs, injustices, and challenges of those around us are complex. How do we as Christians respond when such situations seem so out of control?

True Fasting

What are we to do in a world so full of needs? Certainly, the service of Christ can offer hope and help, but how do we get there? These were my own questions as I began to take inventory of life in the 1980s and 1990s and as I talked more with God and with others about what I could do to break free of a self-centered life to try to help those in need. Then I discovered the soothing words of Isaiah 58:6–12, words that powerfully reflect the attitude and rewards of a service-oriented lifestyle. God is speaking throughout the passage, challenging the religious duties of the people and clarifying (through the prophet Isaiah) that superficial obligations of worship don't lead to a changed heart. The fasting they had done was not as important as denying themselves for the sake of another. God makes it clear that he would rather we care for our fellow humans because, by so doing, we care for ourselves and we deepen our relationship with him. The results are astonishing:

> Is not this the kind of fasting [or devotion] I have chosen:
> to loose the chains of injustice
>> and untie the cords of the yoke,
>> to set the oppressed free
>> and break every yoke?
> Is it not to share your food with the hungry
>> and to provide the poor wanderer with shelter—
> when you see the naked, to clothe him,
>> and not to turn away from your own flesh and blood?
> Then your light will break forth like the dawn,
>> and your healing will quickly appear;
> then your righteousness will go before you,
>> and the glory of the LORD will be your rear guard.
> Then you will call, and the LORD will answer;
>> you will cry for help, and he will say: Here am I.
> If you do away with the yoke of oppression,
>> with the pointing finger and malicious talk,
> and if you spend yourselves in behalf of the hungry
>> and satisfy the needs of the oppressed,
> then your light will rise in the darkness,
>> and your night will become like the noonday.
> The LORD will guide you always;

> he will satisfy your needs in a sun-scorched land
>   and will strengthen your frame.
> You will be like a well-watered garden,
>   like a spring whose waters never fail.
> Your people will rebuild the ancient ruins
>   and will raise up the age-old foundations;
> you will be called Repairer of Broken Walls,
>   Restorer of Streets with Dwellings.

ISAIAH 58:6-12

The more I read this, the more I began to realize that the mysterious principles found in such an eloquent passage are essential to our understanding of the role of service in a balanced life. Why is it that when we spend ourselves on "behalf of the hungry and satisfy the needs of the oppressed" that our own light rises, our own healing occurs? What is it about giving to others that helps us in our own situations? How is it possible that when we offer ourselves on behalf of those in need, the Lord promises to "guide us always" and satisfy our *own* needs and strengthen *our* frames? Perhaps this liberating truth changes us from the inside out, especially when we move beyond our small, self-focused worlds and enter the greater place where human need and divine help intersect. Perhaps there is personal transformation as we connect with both human suffering and holy compassion. As Henri J. Nouwen put it, "The mystery of God's love is not that he takes our pains away, but that he first wants to share them with us. Out of this divine solidarity comes new life."[2]

The more I asked God to help me live out "true fasting," the more I experienced the healing Isaiah 58 proclaims. In other words, the more I volunteered to tutor an inner-city child, the softer I noticed my heart became and the more I appreciated my own education. As I offered to drive my car-less neighbor to the grocery store, the more I began to value the important role daily duties can play in building friendships. And the more I began to strike up conversations with low-income families on my block, the more they taught me about love, loyalty, and forgiveness. Certainly, none of my "deeds" were extraordinary or praiseworthy, but what happened in the process to me personally was amazing: My "frame" became stronger, lighter, while clarity and direction became more real to me than I ever imagined. I don't know exactly when or how I began to feel less self-centered and more concerned about the needs of others. And those close to me will tell you I have a lot to learn and a long, long way to go. I just know that the mysterious reality of Isaiah 58, that is, that our own healing comes when we seek to help others, has begun to change me.

I've discovered this healing aspect of service in others, too, as I've written about urban ministries and unique contemporary servants for a variety of Christian publications. There's the congregation in a Midwestern city that has served its neighbors by offering free veterinarian services one Saturday of every season. They've discovered pet owners can often be low-income, elderly, and lonely neighbors in need of both a friend and a hand with their much-loved animal companions. Yet, it's the Christian vets and church volunteers who have commented on how much they've grown since their Saturday pet-care involvement. There's the suburban women who've organized "mission trips with a purpose" to introduce wealthy women to working women in developing countries and have formed business partnerships and mutual friendships that reach across cultural and economic gaps. There's the former gang member who now pastors the church he initially "wrote off" with tough street talk and who helps other young people in his community. His own transformation came the more he recognized the pains of the teens he now works with. There are the thousands of volunteers who've helped rebuild lives

93

(their own and their neighbors) as they've rebuilt homes for Habitat for Humanity; the Christian families who've become closer to each other since they've relocated to economically depressed neighborhoods to open businesses there; the youth groups whose hearts have grown since they've begun going door to door offering free lawn care or house painting just to show their neighbors they care. If service is about anything, it is about stories such as these that visibly demonstrate to an often hopeless world the love of Christ. In the process, the "ancient ruins" have been rebuilt, the light has risen, and the garden has been well watered for all involved.

I like how Dorothy Day wrote about it: "Love and ever more love is the only solution to every problem that comes up. If we love one another enough, we will bear with each other's faults and burdens. If we love enough, we're going to light that fire in the hearts of others. And it is love that will burn out the sins and hatreds that sadden us. It is love that will make us want to do great things for each other. No sacrifice or suffering will seem too much."[3]

Consider some creative ways you and/or your church could reach out to your community to demonstrate Christ's serving love. How do you think it might help you?

Micah's Mandate

If Isaiah 58 shows us the personal rewards that come from a creative life of service with Christ, Micah 6:8 gives us a daily strategy for acts of giving. Like Isaiah, the prophet Micah was concerned about the empty duties his people were offering to God. They thought they could earn his favor by such religious acts as offering their animals, even their children, as sacrifices to the Lord. Surely, the Almighty would be pleased with such sacrificial deeds, wouldn't he?

No, he would not. Instead, he answers their silly justification with this: "He has showed you, O man, what is good. And what does the LORD require of you? To act justly and to love mercy and to walk humbly with your God" (Micah 6:8). Micah's mandate of justice, mercy, and humility with God helps direct us to radical, balanced discipleship. And each phrase of the Lord's requirement is equally important.

But let's face it, justice is an ignored topic among many North American Christians. I've rarely heard of a Christian seminar on justice or listened to many sermons on it. Occasionally, we hear about a just God, but seldom are we instructed about how we can live out justice in the face of daily injustices. Perhaps justice seems too daunting of a goal for us in the 1990s when the world is so full of civil unrest, war, political power plays, and corporate injustices. Maybe we're just not sure how, if at all, it fits in with our schedules of worship, evangelism, and Bible study. We will stand up every now and then for a neatly packaged fight against, say, an injustice done to unborn babies or children whom we think should be able to pray in public schools. Yet, often our quest for justice ends as a onetime cause; it does not enter our lifestyles.

However, Micah claims justice—that is, "fairness, conformity to moral principles or law, right conduct, merited reward or punishment"—is what the Lord requires of us; it is a nonnegotiable in the Christian life. Though our American history indicates a predominantly voiceless church in regard to justice issues, there are certain issues of justice we cannot ignore any longer: racism, economic discrepancies, religious persecution, sexism, anti-immigrant attitudes, political oppressions, all of which are rampant in our country but extend far beyond our shores. Our spiritual commitment is seen in the justice we do; the sacrifice we do apart from the Holy Spirit or our covenantal relationship with him is what I call "Peace Corps-good," human effort at best, temporary and valuable for a time. Yet, biblical justice goes beyond this and pertains to establishing a relationship that gives back what is due *and beyond that,* as one is able, to deliver the oppressed and to call into account the oppressor.

During his time on earth, Jesus was about bringing justice to a world that had long oppressed and abused people based on their differences, especially those living on the edge of society—the poor, the outcast, the ethnically diverse. His life on earth and his work through the cross brought deliverance to those trapped in oppressed systems or lifestyles. As Waldron Scott said in his book, *Bring Forth Justice,* "The arrival of the Kingdom is the beginning of a radical reversal in the world order, a restoration of justice. . . . To be a disciple is to be committed to the King and his kingdom of just relationships."[4]

The Bible also is full of examples depicting what this kingdom of justice might look like. Deuteronomy 24:17: "Do not deprive the alien or the fatherless of justice, or take the cloak of the widow as a pledge." Leviticus 19:15: "Do not pervert justice; do not show partiality to the poor or favoritism to the great, but judge your neighbor fairly." Psalm 82:3: "Defend the cause of the weak and fatherless; maintain the rights of the poor and oppressed." Jeremiah 22:16: "'He defended the cause of the poor and needy, and so all went well. Is that not what it means to know me?' declares the LORD." Proverbs 21:13: "If a man shuts his ears to the cry of the poor, he too will cry out and not be answered." Proverbs 31:8–9: "Speak up for those who cannot speak for themselves, for the rights of all who are destitute. Speak up and judge fairly; defend the rights of the poor and needy." Justice then becomes our daily vision, or the goal for living out our faith.

And mercy is the way to accomplish it. Why? Because living out justice is not about taking sides, being competitive or argumentative with someone with whom we disagree. Most often, in fact, it is becoming a peacemaker, which inherently requires mercy, or as the Hebrew word for mercy, *hesed,* connotes: "at one and the same time faithfulness, love, mercy and grace; it describes the unfailing love, the keeping of faith between related parties."[5] Almost always, it will cost us something, as it did Jesus. And when we commit to a discipleship that pursues justice, we're going to be given more responsibility, more opportunities, and, consequently, we'll most likely experience more pain, all of which are the components of crossbearing, godly compassion, and mercy.

Mercy, then, should be patterned after God's mercy as revealed through the Bible. It should not be confused with pity. Our role is simply to reflect his mercy, to show compassion and dignity to those in pain. And compassion is never a remote suffering. It makes the first move, risks and freely gives, becomes vulnerable and personally involved. With justice as its goal, mercy cares for the needs of those who have been wronged; it is reflecting God's compassion, or the visible outworking of his love. It is not rationed or conditional compassion based on what we think someone might deserve; God never gave us what we deserved, so we ought to treat others the same.

All Christians should reflect such mercy, though, of course, some might be uniquely gifted for specific acts of mercy or kindness. If that's the case, how do those of us "ordinary" Christians get a merciful heart? Almost always, it comes as a result of personal brokenness or humility before God; without it, we will have no social concern for justice or mercy. We give to the poor because we realize we are poor; we help others in their brokenness and pain because we ourselves are broken and hurt. We help meet another's needs because we ourselves have needs, needs that need to be met. We stand up for one who's been wronged because Christ stood up for us. Anything else is arrogant and superficial, self-indulgent obligation—religious duties that God rebukes, as Isaiah and Micah remind us. Mercy helps us remember that Christ was the Suffering Servant "who for the joy set before him endured the cross, scorning its shame, and sat down at the right hand of the throne of God" (Heb. 12:2). That's why merciful identification with justice as the goal is the most essential (and Christlike) component to biblical service. Empty of self, we enter the world of another human being, ready to learn and eager to be filled with God's overflowing and healing love.

Listen how the Bible reflects this principle: "For I desire mercy, not sacrifice, and acknowledgment of God rather than burnt offerings" said the prophet Hosea (6:6). "Blessed are the merciful, for they will be shown mercy," said Jesus in Matthew 5:7. And again in Matthew 18:33 he said, "Shouldn't you have had mercy on your fellow servant just as I had on you?" Finally, his charge to the religious leaders of his time in Matthew 23:23 relates to us today: "Woe to you, teachers of the law and Pharisees, you hypocrites! You give a tenth of your spices—mint, dill and cummin. But you have neglected the more important matters of the law—justice, mercy and faithfulness." Clearly, God is not impressed with our religious acts; he is delighted, however, when our hearts are focused on justice and our lives reflect his mercy.

What examples of justice and mercy have you seen in your life lately?

As important as these words—*justice* and *mercy*—are, the most important word in the Micah mandate is *with*. Again, it implies relationship. And that is the most crucial element in service: our individual relationship *with* God through Jesus Christ. As much as we should pursue justice with a heart of mercy, it is essential to recognize that Micah's mandate includes another "and" phrase: "and walk humbly with your God." This is the secret to a lifestyle of service that reflects justice and mercy. Otherwise, our deeds, however merciful and just they may be, become mere religious duties, empty sacrifices that God hardly notices. Apart from him, we can do nothing.

So we are to walk humbly *with* our God as we live out these qualities. When we consider all that the Maker has said about himself in his Word, it is not difficult to be humbled. After all, he is Creator (Gen. 1:1), Almighty (Gen. 35:11), jealous (Exod. 34:14), holy (Lev. 19:2), merciful (Deut. 4:31), faithful (Deut. 7:9), the God of Israel (Josh. 24:23), Rock (1 Sam. 2:2), Savior (1 Chron. 16:35), our leader (2 Chron. 13:12), beyond our understanding (Job 36:26), present (Ps. 14:5), my joy and my delight (Ps. 43:4), our refuge and strength (Ps. 46:1), flawless (Prov. 30:5), Wonderful Counselor (Isa. 9:6), a God of justice (Isa. 30:18), true (Jer. 10:10), gracious and compassionate (Jonah 4:2), good (Luke 18:19), the Word made flesh (John 1:1), the builder of everything (Heb. 3:4), our Father (James 1:27), and love (1 John 4:16).

This is the God with whom we walk daily! He is the one whom Micah goes on to tell the Israelites in 7:18, "Who is a God like you, who pardons sin and forgives the transgression of the remnant of his inheritance? You do not stay angry forever but delight to show mercy." Recognizing his mercy, and even a few of his other attributes, automatically humbles us and yet draws us more into his presence. Why? Because, "the LORD said, 'I will cause all

99

my goodness to pass in front of you, and I will proclaim my name, the LORD, in your presence. I will have mercy on whom I will have mercy, and I will have compassion on whom I will have compassion'" (Exod. 33:19). Therefore, we will become merciful, more just, when we stay *with* the one who delights in such mercy and whose character exudes such justice.

A World Watches

So when we respond in mercy to those in need, when we pursue justice as the goal, when we do both out of our humble walk with God, nurturing our solitary fellowship with him, then the unbelieving world pays attention. It is literally dying to witness our authentic, self-sacrificing service with Christ. It notices extraordinary acts of kindness.

Consider the wonderful example of eighty-seven-year-old Oseola McCarty. In 1995, she surprised the nation when she donated $150,000 to the University of Southern Mississippi to establish a scholarship fund for black students. The school often received donations of this size, so what was the big deal? Simple: Miss McCarty earned the money from washing clothes for local residents during the past seventy-five years. Instead of owning a big house or buying new clothes, she saved her money because she just wanted to "help black kids get an education." Her gift stimulated a nationwide response of over thirty-three thousand dollars in additional contributions, and her sense of "making things right" even sparked a letter from the president for her "unselfish deed . . . a remarkable example of the spirit and ingenuity that made America great."

"I'm glad I paid my donation to them," said the laundry woman, who claimed her only education was from the Bible. "If I had any more, I'd give it to them too."

A modern-day good Samaritan? Exactly. In Luke 10:30–37, Jesus esteemed the Samaritan, a poor, social outcast, as an example for living a lifestyle of service, of the Micah mandate, if you will. Samaritans were lower-class citizens primarily because they were utterly despised by the Jews and rejected by the religious leaders of their time. But who was it in the parable who stopped to help the man beaten by robbers and left to die? Not the superspiritual priests or the wealthy Levites, but a Samaritan. Then Jesus said to the expert of the law, "Go and do likewise" (v. 37). In Luke 21:1–4, it was not the rich whom Jesus held up as an example of giving, but the poor widow who "out of her poverty put in all she had to live on."

In turn, God receives glory and the world pricks up its hopeless heart. The commands to serve and to love are not burdensome but rather joyous occasions for bringing a bit of heaven to a hell-bound earth, a morsel of food to a starving world, a touch of love to a lonely person. Indeed, it is when we serve that we most look like Christ. And when we do, the unbelieving world watches.

Review John 13:34–35 and Acts 20:24. What do these passages have to say about what happens when we serve?

The world waits to see faith in action, the witness of Christ's love in daily acts of service. Such deeds could

come at an important time in our nation's history, helping restore the credibility of Christ's church, a credibility that is admittedly tainted and questioned. People in
the 1990s are still skeptical of religious rhetoric, cynical
of so-called "Christian" promises. In a 1995 survey, researcher
George Barna concluded that 71 percent of American
adults believe there is no such thing as absolute truth, a
view shared by 64 percent of people who call themselves
Christians. Apparently, people have become so disillusioned by the fall of Christian leaders and the virtual inac-
tivity of the evangelical church during the past forty years
that they don't think absolute truths exist, let alone firm
foundations for living a life of compassionate service.

I believe it is precisely their lack, though, that has made
them all the more hungry to see Christ in action, providing a perfect opportunity for servants to share the good
news of God's redemptive love. The general public is starving for something certain; offering hope in an act of service becomes the evidence they need to believe. Evangelism at its best comes in actions *and* words, deeds *and*
prayers, practical help *and* altar calls. Why? Because this
same unbelieving world wants desperately to *see* Christ in
action, to experience love in a cup of cold water, hope in
a hand extended to the lonely.

My friend Georgia is living proof. For years, she worked
as an AIDS and cancer specialist at Denver General Hospital in Colorado's capital. Often she would visit patients
in their final days, taking homemade muffins to them
and singing Broadway show tunes to lift their spirits.
She'd tell them stories, too, of the homeless guys she'd
bring to her church in downtown Denver, the stupid
jokes they'd pass her way. She'd recount Sunday's sermon to her patients, play a Christian teaching tape for
them, or teach them Bible verses or worship songs. Every
Christmas she took brand-new socks and underwear to

the homeless shelters, joined her church worship team at the hospices to sing carols, and sent Christmas cards and homemade jam to families of patients who had recently died.

Then a city ordinance got in the way of her work; it required all city employees to live within Denver proper or else run the risk of losing their jobs. Georgia lived barely a few miles beyond city limits but spent all her waking hours in the heart of Colorado's capital, caring for some of its most indigent residents. Still, Georgia was "violating" the law and after ten years of devoted service at the hospital, she was about to lose her employment.

That's when an amazing thing happened. The local weekly alternative newspaper, by far the most militant and liberal media in the city that (as far as I saw) rarely had anything nice to say about anyone, got wind of Georgia's dilemma and decided to do something about it. They wrote a huge story about her, printed her picture on the cover, and defended her as a "great example of Christian living." They quoted her talking about her faith in Jesus, cited her ministry to AIDS patients and homeless people, and even spoke kindly of the evangelical church she attended. "To lose Georgia would be a terrible loss for Denver General," they said.

Imagine this: a non-Christian, politically liberal, anti-religious newspaper putting a Christian woman on its cover! Only one thing explains it: Georgia's attitude as a Christian servant caught the attention—and respect—of these unbelieving journalists. They discovered someone who did more than talk about Christ; they saw him in her consistent acts of kindness. This Christian woman had so penetrated the city with her salt and light that a cynical weekly publication applauded her efforts and rose to her defense. Why? Because the world wants to see faith in action, Jesus with skin on.

The Least of These

Those friends and foes of ours who might not share the same faith in Christ are waiting, watching, hoping they will see something that touches the needs of those around us. In its simplest form, then, service often means looking at your gifts, getting with God, and walking out the door with both to offer a caring solution. For Georgia, it was nursing and singing for those experiencing great pain. For an artist, it might be leading an art class at a local senior center. For an accountant, it might mean offering a few extra hours to a nonprofit ministry to help with the books. Whatever our gift, using it *with* God for the sake of others helps us retain our spiritual balance in a world sorely in need of such a witness. Hundreds of ordinary Christian servants, past and present, have made extraordinary contributions to the world because they have become what some consider the least: ordinary servants taking care of even the most basic of daily, physical needs. They have imitated Christ, and their actions have simply reflected an attitude of wanting desperately to love God with their lives. To those who don't know such love, that is a curious thing to watch.

And it is exactly what will be called into account on judgment day. There are not many places in the Bible that discuss what the day of reckoning will look like, but Matthew 25:31–46 gives us an astounding eternal perspective on our earthly service. Jesus has just been teaching a series of parables on what the kingdom of heaven might be like. Then when he gets to the day of his return, he tells how "all the nations will be gathered before him, and he will separate the people one from another as a shepherd separates the sheep from the goats. He will put the sheep on his right and the goats on his left." Those who are blessed with the "inheritance, the kingdom prepared for you since the creation of the world" will be those who fed the hungry Christ, who gave drink to the thirsty Christ, who invited Christ, the stranger, in, and who visited the sick or prisoner Christ. Those who will be forced to depart from God's presence "into the eternal fire prepared for the devil and his angels" will be those who did not feed, give drink to, invite, or visit the needy Christ. Why? "I tell you the truth, whatever you did not do for one of the least of these, you did not do for me. Then they will go away to eternal punishment, but the righteous to eternal life."

Christ so identifies with the physical needs of the hurting and outcast that he literally takes on their pain, their hunger, their thirst. And if we fail to respond to them, we fail to respond to him. So when we feed a homeless family, give a cup of water to a thirsty neighbor child, visit a dying friend in a hospice or an inmate at the county jail, we are serving Jesus. It is Jesus we meet in the act of such human service, and it is Jesus who works *with* us in providing such help. And it is Jesus who has secured our eternal relationship with him, not our compassionate deeds. But it is our lives of faith, our response to the least of these that reflects our love for him. We will want to love him by loving others. We will rejoice to serve him as we serve others. It will be for us both a life-giving and life-changing relationship.

Yet, in the process, we will also recognize that Jesus never did more than he saw the Father doing, as the apostle wrote in John 5:19. His responses to people's needs always, and only, came out of his intimacy with his heavenly Father, always motivated by the purest form of selfless love possible (1 John 4:8). A careful look at the Gospels will show us that Christ, in fact, did not heal every sickness or eliminate every pain he came in contact with. Why? Because of his intimate union with his Father. This is the secret to living like Christ and responding only as he would; otherwise, it is easy to feel overwhelmed with the many and varied needs of those around us. If we are not being directed by his Spirit, listening to his voice, reflecting on his Word, we will serve and serve and serve, leading us down a tired, bitter road where eventually we burn out entirely.

What does the Lord require of us? To do the right thing and to show compassion and to walk in humility *with* our God. Like Christ, our lives of service must be motivated by our reception of God's eternal love and character, our love for him, and our intimacy with him. When this happens, a whole new world opens before us, one filled with creative opportunities in which an attitude of service can be expressed in actions of help and hope. But we must not think for a minute that we can serve without some help from others. We need people, we need community.

Think about how you can make a personal response to some injustice, whether it's deciding how to be nice to that nasty neighbor, fighting for the rights of low-income families in your city, or helping eliminate world hunger. You might want to explore existing local ministries and how your family could get involved or duplicate one. Ask God to lead you and to give you his heart for justice, mercy, and service.

6

COMMUNITY: SHARING THE MEAL

Vox populi, vox Dei. *The voice of the people is the voice of God.*

ALCUIN, LETTER TO CHARLEMAGNE, A.D. 800

In his short story "The Three Hermits," the great Russian writer Leo Tolstoy tells a tale of a religious Bishop and three hermits. The Bishop is traveling by sea aboard a vessel en route to the Solovetsk Monastery when one day as he walks the deck, he overhears a group of sailors and a fisherman talking about a nameless island where three hermits live.

The sailors point to a tiny dot on the horizon and listen as the fisherman discusses its three inhabitants: "One is a small man and his back is bent. He wears a priest's cassock and is very old; he must be more than a hundred, I should say. He is so old that the white of his beard is taking a greenish tinge, but he is always smiling, and his face is as bright as an angel's from heaven. The second is taller, but he also is very old. He wears a tattered peasant coat. His beard is broad, and of a yellowish grey color. He is a strong man. Before I had time to help him, he turned my boat over as if it were only a pail. He too is kindly and cheerful. The third is tall, and has a beard as white as snow and reaching to his knees. He is stern, with overhanging eyebrows; and he wears nothing but a piece of matting tied around his waist."

Intrigued by what he is hearing, the Bishop asks for more. He is told of the men's silence, of their understanding glances to one another, and of the eldest's only comment, "Have mercy upon us." Legend has it that the hermits live on the island for the salvation of their souls, the sailors chime in. With that, the Bishop convinces the captain to take him ashore so he may minister to the three. He is quickly welcomed by the three silent hermits as he tells them his mission. They smile and listen and glance at each other, but they do not respond. When the Bishop asks how they serve God on this island, the ancient one finally answers: "'We do not know how to serve God. We only serve and support ourselves, servant of God.' 'But how do you pray to God?' asked the Bishop. 'We pray in this way,' replied the hermit. 'Three are ye, three are we, have mercy upon us.' And when the old man said this, all three raised their eyes to heaven, and repeated: 'Three are ye, three are we, have mercy upon us!'"

The Bishop then explains to them the "proper" way to pray to God, acknowledging that clearly they have heard of the Holy Trinity, but, well, they need a little help to get it right. For the next few hours, he tries to teach them the Lord's

Prayer, but they can barely get past "Our Father." Finally, it is getting dark and the Bishop returns to the vessel, pleased that his holy efforts to teach these poor, lonely outcasts have at least provided them with the correct way to pray.

Just as the moon is shining across the water, the Bishop and the sailors notice something coming toward the ship, *atop* the water. Terrified, the men finally recognize what is approaching them: three old men, beards swaying in the wind, gliding across the water without moving their feet!

"We have forgotten your teaching, servant of God. As long as we kept repeating it we remembered. But when we stopped saying it for a time, a word dropped out, and now it has all gone to pieces. Teach us again." All three plead with the Bishop from the water, as with one voice. He, of course, is humbled by their faith and ability to walk on the water, lowers his head, and tells the godly men that their "prayer will reach the Lord. It is not for me to teach you. Pray for us sinners." With that, the men turn and go back across the sea. "And a light shone until daybreak on the spot where they were lost to sight."[1]

Pause and spend a few minutes pondering Tolstoy's story and its possible themes.

Tolstoy's parable is rich with treasures to mine as we begin to look at our third spiritual food group essential for balanced living: community. At the heart of this story (and at the heart of our lives) is the instinctive and universal leaning toward relationships. Yes, they are called hermits, but the three men on the island have a very real sense of what community is: They know each other well enough to speak without words and to interact according to their unique gifts without misunderstanding, just as a family does when it sits down to share a meal. Though the religious missionary tries to teach them the pious ways of Christian devotion, the hermits already understand the triune relationship of Father, Son, and Holy Spirit, perhaps because of their own life together. "Three are ye, three are we, have mercy upon us," is all they know to plead. Yet, it is enough for these three characters to become endearing symbols, symbols Tolstoy uses to confront the possibility of synthetic, mundane, isolated religion. Why? Because the hermits' faith in God is uncluttered, honest, miraculous even, and, as a result, their dependence on each other is pure, real, and unwavering. Both are the heart of Christian community.

Joined Together

If service is the fruit of our solitary fellowship with the Almighty, community is the backdrop or context for both. We cannot live without it. If we volunteer, help, or serve apart from the fellowship and encouragement of other Christians, we can quickly burn out, grow bitter, and do little good for God's kingdom. On the other hand, if we stay in solitude, withdrawn from the presence and support of others, we can be overcome by the paralyzing ache of isolation and loneliness. In short, as the three hermits needed one another for their very survival both physically and spiritually, so, too, do we need people to spur us on in our faith and to help us maintain our balance on the road to salvation.

The root of the word *community* is *comm*, which comes from the Latin *communitas*, as in, common. It literally means "to join together." To understand the importance of community for a balanced, vibrant life, we need only to examine other words with the same root: communion, communication, commune, commute, even communism, which suggests the "common people should own all property and means of production." All of these words imply some sort of joining together. For instance, when we take the communion elements, we are joining our hearts with God's through the body and blood of his Son; when we communicate with friends or family, we are joining emotions and meanings with another's use of language and listening; when we think of a commune, we think of a group of people who have forsaken the ways of the world to join their lives together. And when we commute from the suburbs to the city, we are joining the two "worlds" together.

Community, then, is a coming together, a joining with other flesh and blood that all humans in all cultures in all times of history have found critical for their very existence. It is not merely coexisting beside another person, with no interaction or relation. When sprinters line up for a race in a track meet, for example, they are not displaying any sense of community with one another. Sure, they are standing next to one another, waiting anxiously for the gun to start the race, but merely lining up next to someone with no acknowledgment of the other's humanity or commonality does not constitute community. If at the end of the event, the runners embrace, shake hands, or congratulate one another, then something that looks like what we would call community might have begun.

In its simplest form, then, community requires some sort of connection or common association with others. It is an exchange of dignity that comes in a variety of forms. We might feel a sense of community with those who grew up in the same town as we did, with those who embrace the same political values, or even with those who cheer for the same team. Remember the old television series *Cheers* about a community of misfits who felt "connected" at the neighborhood bar? Its theme song talked about how we all want to go where everyone knows our name. It's no secret that we all long for a sense of acceptance and camaraderie with others, regardless of the setting.

Yet, community also can be created, of course, according to our heritage, ethnicity, or vocation. Whatever the focus of connection, whatever it is that brings people together, the point is that clans, tribes, bloodlines, families, people groups, and cultures of every land throughout history have relied on life-giving, mutual relationships for the sustenance of their emotional, spiritual, and physical livelihood. Community translates into many terms; one Internet search I did revealed more than a dozen such synonyms: alliance, balance, branch, body, church, citizenry, class, collaboration, colony, company, concert, concord, cooperative, denomination, dwellers, everyone, family, fellowship, good vibes, harmony, inhabitants, kibbutz, kinship, likemindedness, mutuality, nationality, oneness, order, populace, public, reciprocity, resemblance, school, sharecropping, society, solidarity, symphony, synergy, teamwork, union, world, you and me. Our national motto in the United States even reflects this idea of common purpose in the midst of individuality: *E Pluribus Unum*, which is Latin for "from many, one."

So we know that community as both word and concept implies more than one person, a plural unit of individuals who are joined together around a common element. Though community might take on different names, it means essentially the same thing: relationships. Regardless of our belief system, culture, or economic status, we cannot survive, or thrive, without them. Why? Because inherent in our humanity is a need to be in life-giving relationships with others. Consequently, community becomes the watering or tilling process that shapes us from the time we are born until the time our hair turns grey and our bones grow frail. Like it or not, parents, siblings, relatives, teachers, friends, enemies, spouses, neighbors all play a part in molding our character and framing our stature. One pastor used to tell his congregation that "we are all just composites of other people." True enough, we cannot live without people who inevitably influence and nurture us, yet the perpetual struggle each of us faces is that too many times we cannot live *with* them! Truth be told, relationships are plain hard work, and they can become unhealthy, imbalanced, or distant particularly if we place unrealistic or unfair expectations on others to meet our needs. Or if we don't have a clear understanding of what community is supposed to be, we can stay self-centered, withdrawn, or mean-spirited.

Take a minute to thank God for the people he has used in your life to shape your character.

Three Are Thee

If relationships are essential to and inherent in our beings, how, then, do we build strong, life-giving, mutual ones that help us keep our spiritual balance? What distinguishes authentic Christian community from these other forms of community? Considering that a Gallup poll recently revealed little difference in lifestyle between those who go to church and those who don't, it is certainly a question worth exploring. We need to look at the nature and heart of the Triune Creator as the starting place for forming our perspective of Christian community. From there we will begin to see that our relationships must reflect his character, and in the process, they will change us, as iron sharpens iron. Indeed, we cannot grow, remain balanced, or influence our culture with the gospel without being intimately involved in each other's lives.

It is no accident that we need each other. In chapter one, we learned that the Latin concept *imago Dei* means we humans are made in God's image. God's whole being as Creator and Author of Life is one that seeks relationship with his created ones. In the Genesis account of creation, we hear God saying, "'Let us make man in our image, in our likeness, and let them rule over fish of the sea and the birds of the air, over the livestock, over all the earth, and over all the creatures that move along the ground.' So God created man in his own image, in the image of God he created him; male and female he created them" (1:26–27). Not only do we see the privilege and precedence God gave humankind over the earth and other creatures, but we see his creative heart expressed in a collective voice. This is not some mythical picture of an old man with a long white beard, rubbing his whiskers, and saying, "Hmm. What shall I concoct now?" In fact, there's no biblical evidence of God the Creator being an individual inventor at all (or of being an old man with a white beard!); note his choice of pronouns is "us" not "me." The three-in-one relationship, that is, the Father, Son, and Holy Spirit, created cooperatively the object of his love: human beings. As one scholar explained it, "The Bible reveals to us: the invisible Father, from whom all revelations proceed; the Son, who mediates and objectively incarnates that revelation as a historical reality; and the Holy Spirit, who is divinely outpoured and subjectively applies that revelation to each of us."[2]

It was around the third century that the Latin term *trinitas*, that is, the state of being threefold, was first applied to what we now recognize as the Christian term of Trinity. Regardless of what we called him before then or since, believers have clung to the unity of God the Father, God the Son, and God the Holy Spirit, holding that the Three

Persons in One are equal in power, different in divine roles, the same in authority. Scholars cite over fifty biblical references to the three-in-one nature of God, and church leaders from many denominations and cultures have esteemed the Holy Trinity by naming their very churches appropriately—Trinity Lutheran and Holy Trinity of London to name a few. The equal roles within the Trinity find common ground among Orthodox Christians and Pentecostals alike. From the prayers of early Christians that often praised the Holy Spirit at the same time they praised God the Father and Christ the Son, to the articles, sermons, and books of contemporary theologians and preachers who explore the unique roles of each God-Person, Christians throughout the ages have found the threefold nature of the Almighty a common, corporate cornerstone.

With good reason: The three present a perfectly balanced sense of order and intent in both divine function and human intervention, a holy, relational triangle, if you will. Some analogies for the Trinity I've heard are that he is like the three water components, ice, steam, and liquid. Or three primary colors reflecting out a single ray of light. Or three tones blending into one chord of music. But these illustrations don't quite communicate the unique qualities of an infinite God to our finite minds. Many Bible scholars, instead, identify the Godhead as three in aspect and manifestation (how they show themselves), but one in quality (they are complete and perfect), substance (whatever it is that makes God God, all three are), purpose (their aim regarding the created universe is the same), and power (all three can do anything). And reduced to its purest message, the gospel, or Good News, of Christ is really about the Trinity: God the Father sent God the Son, Jesus, to invade the earth and invite sinful humans into eternal loving relationship with him through the sacrifice of his death, leaving God the Holy Spirit to fill them with his new life and

115

constant presence. "Exalted to the right hand of God, he has received from the Father the promised Holy Spirit and has poured out what you now see and hear" (Acts 2:33).

Therefore, the Holy Trinity not only reflects God's relational nature but is the foundation for our unifying Christian belief. Perhaps the Nicene Creed, the most widely accepted and used statement of the Christian faith, best communicates the threefold nature of our God. In liturgical churches, it is included every Sunday as part of the common liturgy, with thousands of Christians reciting it together in services throughout the world. It is also a common confession for Eastern Orthodox, Roman Catholics, Anglicans, Lutherans, Presbyterians, and many other Christian groups. Even those congregations who do not use it in their services nevertheless are committed to the doctrines it teaches:

> We believe in one God,
> the Father, the Almighty,
> maker of heaven and earth,
> of all that is, seen and unseen.
> We believe in one Lord, Jesus Christ,
> the only son of God,
> eternally begotten of the Father,
> God from God, Light from Light,
> true God from true God,
> begotten, not made,
> of one being with the Father.
> Through him all things were made.
> For us and for our salvation
> he came down from heaven:
> by the power of the Holy Spirit
> he became incarnate from the Virgin Mary,
> and was made man.
> For our sake he was crucified under Pontius Pilate;
> he suffered death and was buried.
> On the third day he rose again
> in accordance with the Scriptures;

he ascended into heaven
and is seated at the right hand of the Father.
He will come again in glory
to judge the living and the dead,
and his kingdom will have no end.
We believe in the Holy Spirit, the Lord, the giver of life,
who proceeds from the Father [and the Son].
With the Father and the Son
he is worshipped and glorified.
He has spoken through the Prophets.
We believe in one holy catholic and apostolic Church.
We acknowledge one baptism for the forgiveness of sins.
We look for the resurrection of the dead,
and the life of the world to come. Amen.

*Take a few minutes to confess your faith
to God through the Nicene Creed.
What does it teach you about God's nature?*

Three Are We

God's triune character teaches us not only about his mysterious and incredible being, but about ours as well, since
we are created in his image. He is three in one, bonded by
perfect holiness, consistent in purpose for the sake of loving relationship, united in distinctive actions. There is a
wonderful diversity in his unity, a holy uniqueness in his
oneness, and a joyous wholeness in his separateness. The
three are never apart in being, never divided in vision,
never independent of the other in mission. Yet, their intimacy never threatens their identities, nor does it prevent

117

them from accomplishing their purposes for fellowship with us mere mortals.

It is a humbling thing to think of ourselves as reflections of the Master of the Universe, the King of Kings, the Prince of Peace, the Wonderful Counselor. The Triune God communicates to us that our individual lives are never to be apart from the support and fellowship of other Trinity-reflections (that is, other Christians). In spite of what our individualistic society says, our lives do *not* belong to us, just as our faith in him is never for our own sake alone nor does our personal salvation and eternal security suggest we will be dining alone at the heavenly banquet. No, we are created in the image of the One who *is* relationship, and therefore, we are to be about our Father's business in bringing unity on earth in the midst of our human diversity. Self-sufficiency and contemporary Western independence is a myth and contradictory to the example our Creator has set for us in his character.

A single friend of mine recently returned from a short-term mission trip to various parts of northern Africa. Her team visited several Christian churches seeking to care for their neighbors, many of whom have suffered the horrors and injustices of civil war, religious persecution, and (preventable) diseases and famines. One night as she spoke with a few of the Christian workers about their personal lives, my friend talked about her life back home in New York City, how she lived alone in an apartment and worked as an administrative assistant. As soon as she told them about her living situation, her new African friends immediately reacted with sympathy and pity for the American woman. They looked straight into her hazel eyes and whispered, "I'm so sorry you live alone. You don't have any family or friends to help you?"

My friend laughed at their comment and quickly explained how close she is to her family and friends—they just don't happen to live together. But she also recognized that her friends might be on to something. Obviously, the reality of biblical community is much more of a priority in particular cultures around the world than it is in our Western society. Through television sitcoms, advertisements, films, and "modern" lifestyles, we have become a country that too often advocates personal autonomy, self-gratifying materialism, and emotional isolation over the virtues of interdependence, simplicity, and shared living. Yet, those of us who align ourselves with the Triune God and comprise what has been called his church cannot afford to follow our culture down its self-indulgent path.

Perhaps we need to explore more of who we were created to be as the church, to explore a few of the metaphors that help describe who we are as people of God, in order to understand more of who we really are. Tolstoy's hermits humbly referred to themselves as "three are we"; many of us call ourselves Christians (which really means "Little Christ"), Baptists, Catholics, Presbyterians, or a variety of other notable religious titles. I'm not so sure the label matters as much as the way we live out community for the sake of our Servant King and for the sake of those he came to save. Henri J. Nouwen helps clarify that calling as he explains in the following: "The Greek word for church, *ekklesia*—from *ek*=out, and *kaleo*=call—indicates that as a Christian community we are people who together are *called out* of familiar places to unknown territories, out of our ordinary and proper places to the places where people hurt and where we can experience with them our common human brokenness and our common need for healing."[3]

So we are called out of familiar places, and we are broken with a common need for healing. That makes us a part of one another. I have always marveled at the metaphor God gives us in Romans 12:4–5, "Just as each of us has one body with many members, and these members do not all have the same function, so in Christ we who are many form one body, and each member belongs to all the others." And again in 1 Corinthians 12:12–27,

> The body is a unit, though it is made up of many parts; and though all its parts are many, they form one body. So it is with Christ. For we were all baptized by one Spirit into one body—whether Jews or Greeks, slave or free—and we were all given the one Spirit to drink. Now the body is not made up of one part but of many. . . . But in fact God has arranged the parts in the body, every one of them, just as he wanted them to be. If they were all one part, where would the body be? As it is, there are many parts, but one body . . . so that there should be no division in the body, but that its parts should have equal concern for each other. If one part suffers, every part suffers with it; if one part is honored, every part rejoices with it. Now you are the body of Christ, and each one of you is a part of it.

If God equates Christians as literal members of the same body (his!), it seems to me our connection, commitment, and mission to (and with) each other ought to be a whole lot more cohesive than it seems to be in our contemporary society. Think of how intricate the human body is, how its muscles and tendons hold together bones and support joints, how blood keeps life flowing through veins and arms and toes, how nerves communicate pain and danger, how organs filter wastes and infections. Modern medicine continues to be baffled at how some parts of the body function naturally to fight off disease, or why certain miracles occur within the body itself at all. The human body is certainly one of the most powerful analogies the apostle Paul could have chosen to communicate God's passion for community; it is almost as intricate and as unfathomable as the Holy Trinity.

But let's be honest: We usually view these passages more as nice Christian images than as actual biblical mandates. For instance, do we really allow those we know are "hands" and "feet" in our congregations to work together? Do we really seek to avoid even the appearance of division in the body? Do we really see ourselves as one body, regardless of how different other parts might look racially, culturally, or economically? Do we really suffer when other parts are suffering? Or do we withdraw when things get too uncomfortable or messy, so focused on our own lives and comfort that we've dismissed the identity that God's given us as his body? And if we really continue to carry the metaphor of the body, why is it that too many wounded Christians are no longer in fellowship with one another? Perhaps because as John Stott said, "The Church is both the guardian of the truth and very prone to error. The Church is both the holy people of God and a motley bunch of sinners. The Church is both united and disunited. I'm sure God says to Himself, 'I have only one Church, the body of my Son, although these human beings have succeeded in splintering and splitting it a good deal.'"

Yes, dismembered parts of Jesus lie all over the streets of our cities and communities.

Ask God to show you specific brothers and sisters who have been wounded by other parts of the body, who are feeling cut off from fellowship and Christian friendship. Maybe you yourself are feeling this way right now. Ask God to bring healing to his body.

Paul also writes in Ephesians 2:21–22 about how in Christ "the whole building is joined together and rises to become a holy temple in the Lord. And in him you too are being built together to become a dwelling in which God lives by his Spirit." Not only are we his body, but we are his temple, the dwelling of the Trinity himself, a building that reflects to others his attributes and holiness. Obviously, no building is made up of one solitary brick; no temple (sanctuary or synagogue) has only one seat. In other words, there is never isolation for the Christian; even in solitude we are never fully alone. Why? Because we are *with* the God and Father of our spiritual brothers and sisters, siblings we immediately "inherited" when we were adopted into the family of God. Community for the Christian, then, is nonnegotiable; we are born into God's family when we come into the life-changing relationship with Christ. Happily, our conversions automatically qualify us to be an integral part of a multinational, multiethnic, multieconomic, and historic community, one with a long, rich biblical heritage, one with unending purpose and possibilities. One of my pastors at Redeemer Presbyterian Church in New York City explained this concept well:

> "A city set on a hill" is a community image, not an individual one. Jesus assumed that there would be visible, concrete communities who by the quality of their corporate life were noticeable and distinct. Jesus and the rest of biblical writers thought of themselves in terms of a community prior to thinking of themselves as individuals. Once we are tuned into that, a reexamination of the Scriptures demonstrates that such corporate imagery dominates. We are the "body of Christ," "a temple of living stones," "a living sacrifice." In fact, the promise which is at the heart of the Bible—"I will be your God and you will be my people"—is nothing less than God's promise to build us into a community in which he himself is the chief participant. The purpose of God's saving work in Christ Jesus is not the rescuing of separate individuals who remain relatively unconnected. Instead, the purpose of his saving work is the formation of a people, a new family over which he presides as Father. Community is the goal of the gospel.[4]

Watching Your Back

In many U.S. urban neighborhoods, the phrase "I got your back!" means that a friend is looking out for a friend, a neighbor is supporting a neighbor. For instance, if danger seems to be lingering around the corner, a friend's proclamation of "I got your back!" means there is protection, safety, and help from one who cares about you. The mere announcement is good news for the person who is feeling threatened or trapped in a potentially vulnerable position.

So it should be for us in the Christian community who are created in the image of the Triune Almighty. Our corporate life should communicate good news to others, as we reflect a concern and support like that of our Maker. Together, we should seek opportunities to serve, uplift, encourage, and pray for one another and for those in need. When we learn to take care of one another, to carry one another's burdens, we experience the heart of our Savior who laid down his life for his friends, the one who is always saying to us, "I got your back!"

If we sincerely know that we belong to each other as, say, a hand belongs to an arm, when we deeply understand that our lives are mirrors of the Creator whose entire nature pursues our friendship, when we repent for our self-sufficiency and inability to admit our need for one another, and when we commit ourselves to others as we commit to Christ, then living out our mandate for community will solidify our balanced spiritual lives, and, in the process, invite others to the King. Because, "surely entrance into the Christian Church presupposes total commitment to Christ as the Lord of the church. A surrender to Christ is a surrender to His people—total involvement in the life of the church and the awareness that participation in this community of forgiveness and love means that we must extend it to all mankind," wrote Elizabeth O'Connor in her book *Call to Commitment*.[5]

123

But it's one thing to recognize and receive our identity and purpose as a community of fellow believers, created in our Father's image, for the sake of personal and corporate nourishment and balance. It is quite another to allow that identity to spill over into our lifestyles.

Write in your prayer journal about those Christian brothers and sisters who have been community to you. Pray for them now.

7

COMMUNITY:
EATING TOGETHER

"It doesn't happen all at once," said the Skin Horse. "You become. It takes a long time. That's why it doesn't often happen to people who break easily, or have sharp edges, or who have to be carefully kept. Generally by the time you are Real, most of your hair has been loved off, and your eyes drop out and you get loose in the joints and very shabby. But these things don't matter at all, because once you are Real you can't be ugly, except to people who don't understand."

MARGERY WILLIAMS, *THE VELVETEEN RABBIT*

When I was growing up, my mom would often cook huge dinners for Thanksgiving, Easter, and Christmas. She'd spend hours in the kitchen for days before the holiday feast, preparing turkeys or hams, slicing potatoes, baking vegetable casseroles and pumpkin pies. Once the aroma of our much anticipated dinner caught our attention, my brothers and I would set the table, putting knives, forks, and plates in their proper places. Then when it was time to sit down, my mom would call each member of our family to come to the table, take our seat, and dive into the delicious meal she had worked so hard to prepare. After my dad carved the turkey, we'd pass the gravy and stuffing around to one another, the cranberries and rolls, the potatoes and veggies. We'd eat until we had no more room left in our bellies, and then we'd sit at the table together unable to move, satisfied from all we had shared. We were full in every way.

What qualified us to sit at the dining room table for those holiday banquets? The simple fact that we were members of the same family, bearers of the same last name, bonded by common blood and love (especially for food!). Our identity gave us the right to come together, but that didn't mean we could do anything we wanted once we pulled up our chair. We knew we each had a job to fulfill before and after the meal, as well as certain rules to follow in order to enjoy eating together. "Table manners," my mom called them.

So it is with those of us in the Christian community. In the last chapter, we learned of our identity as the family of God, sharers of the same meal, bearers of the common name of the Holy Trinity. We've been invited to participate together in the spiritual feast of solidarity and camaraderie that our Creator has prepared for us, a feast that will certainly nourish us and sustain us. But that does not mean we can do whatever we want when we come to the table of fellowship. It is important for us to recognize that the Master of the house has given us unique roles to play and certain "table manners" to follow, particular guidelines to ensure that we make the most of our time together.

A New Kingdom

Today, I live in a city quite different from the one I grew up in, a city that many believe is one of the most difficult places in the country to form community: New York. Maybe it's the challenges of subways, buses, and honking cabs that make it difficult for people to get together; maybe it's the career-driven schedules that replace social outings with deadlines; maybe it is New York's size and fast pace that keep people from relating with each other. Though over eight million people live in the five-borough metropolitan "kingdom," it's no secret that people here find it difficult to connect with one another. Isolation, loneliness, and anonymity are as common as crowded streets. Christians here have to be particularly intentional and determined to build any sense of community and spiritual fellowship; if they don't, it's simply too easy to fall from the faith and get swept along with the tide of people.

But make no mistake: Christians in New York City in the 1990s are not the only ones who have found it challenging to live out their faith with fellow believers. There was the early church after Christ's crucifixion, the monastic communities of the Middle Ages, the radical sects of the sixteenth and seventeenth centuries, and the revolutionary groups of the 1800s. This century has seen the birth of Catholic Worker Homes or farms, Dietrich Bonhoeffer's Lutheran community in Nazi Germany, countercultural communities such as the Bruderhof movement (in which hundreds of families share a common purse, a justice mission, and a simple Christ-centered lifestyle together in the United States and England), and interracial groups of Chris-

127

tians (like Jesus People USA in Chicago or Harambee Center in Pasadena, California) who have pooled their resources, paychecks, and lives around a common house and ministry. Today, there are church homes, denominational convents, even Christian subdivisions in which congregations invest to meet their housing and community needs.

To be sure, there are hundreds of ways Christians (and non-Christians alike) have attempted to live out a corporate mission and a common lifestyle together. Some (like the ones mentioned above) have lived together intentionally, sharing possessions, food, and friendships in the midst of horrendous times, trying to reflect the triune nature of God and his unifying love during times when the world looked every way but to Christ. Others have withdrawn entirely from their societies into the country or mountains to sustain themselves apart from unbelieving neighbors. Still others have lived side by side in urban areas, meeting together frequently in one another's homes for meals or support as they brought the Good News to the masses.

Our brothers and sisters throughout the centuries have pursued this ideal of community out of both human necessity and biblical conformity. Yet, all have found themselves wanting. Why? Because relationships are hard work. Though sometimes we feel we can't live *with* them, most of the time we feel we can't live *without* them. We long for life-giving, supportive, and accountable relationships with people who share a similar vision or purpose as we do. Yet, often we don't know how to accomplish that. Or we give up in the trying because the going gets too difficult; our emotions, insecurities, and egos get bruised or battered along the way. Of course, deep in our souls, we know—in spite of what our independent Western society bombards us with—we need each other, that relationships are worth the efforts and the risks. We simply cannot make it in this life alone, but the reality is that community relationships can hurt. Certainly, Basil Pennington was right when he said, "The rigorous demands of true friendship, the gift of oneself, one's time, one's preferences, the nakedness and honesty, are beyond the price many are willing to pay—those who have not yet experienced what is purchased by such a price. Anyone who has been graced with true friendship knows the cost and knows the worth."[1]

Solitude births God's character and integrity in us, service helps work it outward, but it is community—the gift of flawed and divinely created human beings—that sharpens, molds, and purifies it. Flint on steel, as one friend calls it, keeping the fire of God's presence alive. Since Christ walked the earth, Christians have been "flint" to one another. None, of course, has formed community perfectly. Indeed, none of us will ever find a perfect church, a perfect marriage or family, or perfect Christian friendships as long as we're in this world of sin and as long as we put our own needs over those of others. Yet, we don't give up on community because our hope lies in the truth that one day God will gather the nations in a place called heaven where we will worship and eat and love together for eternity, in *his* perfect holiness.

Reflect on the promise of a heavenly community. What does that look like to you?

Such a vision is precisely what must spur us on in our relationships. In spite of the challenges we find when relating to one another, we must cling to the command to love God and love our neighbor as ourselves. And we must be creative, reflective, and courageous in how we obey such a twofold command. For instance, one of the first verses I was encouraged to memorize during my early Christian days in high school was the familiar promise of Jesus found in Matthew 6:33: "But seek first his kingdom and his righteousness, and all these things will be given to you as well." At that time in my young materialistic life, I particularly liked the part about "all these *things* will be given to you as well." I figured that if I was obedient in having my ten-minute quiet time most mornings and attending youth group once a week, I'd get some pretty neat stuff!

As I grew, I began to replace the word *kingdom* with *King* in my spiritual understanding, thinking this verse instructed me first to seek after Christ the King and then expect the things to be given me. Certainly, we do need to bring our needs before the Almighty, asking for his help and provision, humbly expecting he will take care of our needs. As we've said throughout these chapters, we must nurture an ongoing solitary fellowship with our Maker if we are to reflect his balanced life. But the older I get, the more I'm beginning to look differently at this favorite old verse altogether, especially considering its context.

This kingdom passage is taken from the Lord's famous Sermon on the Mount in which he addresses a variety of controversial issues as they pertain to his people, his community of believers. This particular section of the sermon shows Christ speaking very specifically about God's ability to provide for our physical sustenance. He encourages us to notice the lilies and the sparrows that the Father created and feeds. We are not to worry about what we are to wear or eat—two of our most basic necessities—for he is more than able to grant them to his children

How does he do that? Through his kingdom. In other words, I wonder if Christ wasn't describing what he imagined his kingdom of believers would look like, a kingdom where no one is in physical need because the King has used his servants to provide care for each other accordingly. Of course, a kingdom is never comprised of just one individual; in fact, a kingdom is "the realm of a king, any society or classification [of people]." It always implies that there is a group of individuals—a community—who together live under the authority and provision of their king or sovereign authority.

Certainly, this was the case with the early church, as Acts 2:44–46 describes: "All the believers were together and had everything in common. Selling their possessions and goods, they gave to anyone as he had need. Every day they continued to meet together in the temple courts. They broke bread in their homes and ate together with glad and sincere hearts." And again in Acts 4:32–35: "All the believers were one in heart and mind. No one claimed that any of his possessions was his own, but they shared everything they had. With great power the apostles continued to testify to the resurrection of the Lord Jesus, and much grace was upon them all. There were no needy persons among them. For from time to time those who owned lands or houses sold them, brought the money from the sales and put it at the apostles' feet, and it was distributed to anyone as he had need."

If we really are the family of God, we will do anything we have to—including something as radical as selling our property—to make sure our spiritual siblings and relatives will have enough food to eat or clothes to wear. When concerned parents consider moving their family to another town, they don't just decide based on their own vocational or emotional desires. They take into account what will ultimately be best for their children—their little kingdom—and then take steps to provide accordingly. So it should be with us. In other words, I can't help but wonder if these passages don't suggest that we seek *first* God's community, and his shared righteousness, for the well-being of all of us. For

131

instance, could they be requiring us to consider the *whole* body of Christ when making any vocational or geographical decisions? Should we first consider what's best for others, for God's entire kingdom, before purchasing this product or pursuing that dream? Doesn't Christ's command lead us to seek first the kingdom, as in, his body, his church, his people, his righteousness, under his kingship and his sovereignty? Isn't his kingdom a group of servants who together acknowledge the King of Kings and attempt to live out their love for God by loving one another with their lives?

I once heard of a well-known California pastor who preached that he felt Christians should never move to another city for the sake of a job but for the sake of a church. He felt if their decision was based first on their careers they might be tempted to forgo the importance of Christian fellowship, reducing it to an idea rather than a vital necessity for the corporate growth and well-being of all involved. An active parishioner listening one Sunday had just been offered a promotion in his job; the only catch was he'd have to move to a city fifteen hundred miles away where he didn't know anyone and he knew of no specific churches. He had struggled with whether he should leave his volunteer ministry roles at the church and the small group Bible study he had been a part of for the past three years. These Christians had become like family to him; how could he leave them simply for a step up the career ladder? Hearing his pastor's counsel, he decided to turn down the promotion so he could retain the essential Christian relationships he had begun.

A fool? Maybe. But a fool for Christ who recognized his role in and need for the body of Christ, and who was not going to allow societal pressures to distract him from either. Obviously, this is a powerful way community can be accomplished, by seeking *first* God's kingdom or family and allowing kingdom values to govern our lifestyle choices. We must reflect a high commitment to Christ's community, then,

132

to ensure both our balanced lives and that "all these things shall be added to us." However, we must not forget that community is not just for our own sakes; sure, we need it to keep us anchored and on target. But we must not forget that God's community needs us as well. In other words, our decisions, experiences, and insights are crucial for the Almighty's bigger picture. God's will for our lives is never just about "little old me." It has a spiritual ripple effect, if you will. What we choose this month, God might use for someone we meet five years from now! Therefore, our vision for community cannot be self-indulgent or immediate; it must be for the sake of Christ's body of fellow believers both now and for the future. When that happens, our personal sense of community begins to mirror particular attributes of the sovereign Trinity.

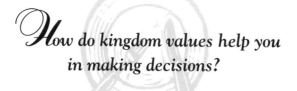

How do kingdom values help you in making decisions?

Looking to Others

If we must maintain a healthy sense of community relationships for one another's good, what must such relationships look like? Perhaps the Velveteen Rabbit gives us our first clue: We have to learn to get real with one another. Getting real with each other takes a long time and a lot of patience, not to mention divine intervention along the way. It will inherently mean that such a road will not always be easy or painfree, especially since we are creatures who are both human and spiritual. But if we commit ourselves

133

to particular kingdom values, then God's triune character will surely surface in our interactions, leading us to fully celebrate our humanity and our Christianity.

To develop a checklist for building such a community we must be willing to offer ourselves to one another as we do our Maker. Why? Because as Julie Gorman says in *Community That Is Christian*,

> How can we love our Father but not His other children? . . . We are called to an inheritance of community. But it is also a call to commit to the realization of this standard and that doesn't just happen. It takes work and patience. Living in community requires cultivation of concepts of mutuality, service, and corporate responsibility. It implies receiving and pursuing, increasing self-disclosure, and interdependency. There is no "lite" relational commitment for those who find it difficult to be in a group relationship. . . . We acknowledge that life is essentially *us* and not just *me*.[2]

By acknowledging that life is *us* and not just *me*, we are committing our lives to one another, to the work and care of all the parts of our Lord's body for the sake of our witness to the world. Christ himself tells us that the whole world will know that we are his disciples if we lay down our lives for and love one another (John 13:35). Consequently, our relationships must speak of a truth, a grace, and a love far greater than our puny selves and agendas. But we are not left to our own to try to live this out; God's Spirit empowers us and works in us that which pleases him most: unity. And thankfully, God's Word provides us with a wonderful blueprint for such an endeavor through a series of "one-anotherisms."

Consider the wonderful admonitions to be at peace with one another (Mark 9:50), to love one another as Christ loved us (John 13:34), to be devoted to one another in love (Rom. 12:10), to stop passing judgments on one another

(Rom. 14:13), to serve one another in love (Gal. 5:13), to be kind and compassionate to one another (Eph. 4:32), to submit to one another (Eph. 5:21), to forgive one another (Col. 3:13), to encourage one another (Heb. 10:25), to confess your sins to one another (James 5:16), to love one another deeply from the heart (1 Peter 1:22), to offer hospitality to one another (1 Peter 4:9), and to have fellowship with one another (1 John 1:7).

Amazingly, God's character is best formed in us in the context of day in day out relationships in which these "one-anotherisms" can be modeled. For instance, our knowledge of Christ's love increases as we give and receive pure, sacrificial love with one another; our insight about God's compassion, kindness, and care deepens as we experience those attributes from other Christians; our sense of God's incredible grace and forgiveness expands and heals us as we receive these gifts from other brothers and sisters through confession. Bonhoeffer explained this well: "When God was merciful to us, we learned to be merciful to our brethren. When we received forgiveness instead of judgment, we, too, were made ready to forgive our brethren. What God did to us, we then owed to others. The more we received, the more we were able to give; and the more meager our brotherly love, the less were we living by God's mercy and love."[3]

Imagine what our world would look like if Christians lived these one-anotherisms out on a regular basis, if we stopped passing judgment on one another, and if we freely offered his care, mercy, and hope to one another. Would our corporate love and hospitality become so attractive that others would want to be invited into our fellowship? Could our commitment to each other inspire a genuine curiosity about the Light of the World while dispelling the deeds of darkness? I think so. True community, after all, is a place of freedom *and* accountability, forgiveness *and* reconciliation, playfulness *and* confession, grace *and* truth, listening *and* speaking. It affirms and develops the unique gifts of each individual not for his own sake but for the strengthening of the whole body. It celebrates the common mission of the gospel for the inclusion of those who might be lost throughout the world. In community, there is unity in diversity, healing in burden-bearing, and common living with eternal vision.

Reflect on a few of the one-anotherisms. What are they communicating to you right now?

Strength in Numbers

When we live well together, that is, when we follow the one-anotherisms of the New Testament, not only is our Lord's compelling presence lifted up for all to see, but the forces of darkness are pushed into hiding. His kingdom is held together, not torn apart. In other words, our authentic community becomes a shield that protects us from the attacks and battles of the evil one. Division is the enemy's greatest gain, unity his greatest fear.

Rarely have I seen this spiritual battle more clearly than in Walter Wangerin Jr.'s 1975 fantasy novel, *The Book of the Dun Cow*. The story revolves around Chauntecleer, a rooster and a reluctant leader, whose domain is a chicken coop filled with talking mice, annoying hens, whining weasels, and a scraggly dog with a bad case of "low self esteem." Their enemy, the evil Wyrm (and symbol of Satan), lives under the earth, trapped by the animals' unity and cohesion. It is Chauntecleer's job to make sure everyone fulfills his or her role by doing what each was created to do. If a hen, to lay eggs. If a dog, to howl and befriend. Why? Because if even the slightest role is out of sync or a division occurs, Wyrm's demons will attack and eventually Wyrm himself will escape from the earth, kill the inhabitants, and "roar almighty challenges to the Lord God Himself." Wangerin even calls Chauntecleer and his motley members of the coop "Wyrm's Keepers"; it is their union that keeps him imprisoned, powerless to wreak his evil havoc on the earth.

But disaster does come—maybe because of the rooster's self-indulgent arrogance—and a battle ensues. After the first encounter with Wyrm's soldiers, Chauntecleer's troops appear badly wounded. He is discouraged, as is his beat-up army scattered before him. Wangerin describes the scenario this way: "The wasted land, the shattered society, the bodies dead and festering, were all great Wyrm's triumph. In one small part of the earth his Keepers had been first weakened and then killed. Their lives, which locked his life beneath the earth; their banded peace, which chained him there; their goodly love, which was his torment; their righteousness, which was iron against his will—that fabric had in one place on the earth been torn."[4]

What happens when Christians don't stand together in unison? The result is "a wasted land, a shattered society where bodies are festering." It doesn't require a great imagination to see that this is exactly what has happened in our Western society, where the body of Christ has replaced "banded peace and goodly love" with selfish desires and deceptive individualism. We have not celebrated one another in the body of Christ. Instead we have competed or complained against others, ignoring the one-anotherisms that could change our world, and consequently, unlocking the horrors of darkness—the "chains and torments" of the devil himself. We have not confessed our sins to one another, rather we have passed judgment. We have shared little of our hearts, let alone our lives or our possessions, and so the evil one has made his claim across the land, replacing God-intended values of sacrificial community and extravagant grace with wicked independence and narcissistic pride.

Wangerin presents the Good News, however, in his book as Chauntecleer gathers his strength and leads his troops to victory—but only because his bloodstained community first rallies around their man (or rooster) and speaks truth to him. Through words, they encourage him to keep going. In their verbal support of their wounded leader, we see the power of community as it touches the invalid and he rises, albeit angry and smarting, but risen nonetheless to fight the dreaded Wyrm and his demons. The message is clear: We are Christ's healers to one another, and only together do we stand a chance against our spiritual foe.

And healing in community almost always comes from the physical presence and the spoken words of God through our fellow human beings. That's why we have to be committed to the value of community-building relationships and, therefore, discipline every aspect of our individual lives around its corporate good. From our solitude and service to our thinking and our words, we must recognize how our attitudes toward one another reflect our relationship with our mutual Father, especially since an enormous battle is at stake. At the center of such preparation is the gift of language.

As Christ was the Word made flesh (John 1:1), and God spoke creation into existence (Genesis 1), so, too, do we have the ability to build a powerful community through our choice of words to one another. Human emotions are wrecked or healed through language—we can build up or tear down through whatever comes out of our mouths to one another. Unfortunately, though, as the apostle James said, "No man can tame the tongue. It is a restless evil, full of deadly poison. With the tongue we praise our Lord and Father, and with it we curse men, who have been made in God's likeness. Out of the same mouth come praise and cursing. My brothers, this should not be" (3:8–10). No indeed! But too often it is our choice of language that creates dissension and bitterness; we say things about Christ's body we ought not to say, and we strike out at those made in God's likeness with words that steal, kill, and destroy. When Christians speak anything but grace toward one another, no wonder the unbelieving world looks away and laughs. All they hear from us is judgment, pride, and wrath. Who wants it?

Yet, the Bible also says that "out of the overflow of his heart his mouth speaks" (Luke 6:45). If our hearts are full of God's grace and forgiveness because of the solitary fellowship we have nurtured with him and because of the service that has called it forth, then our words to one another will speak the same. Essentially, community is built or ruined because of what fills our hearts and then flows out of our mouths and into our ears. We all know too well the stories of fellow Christians who have stopped attending this church or that fellowship group because of the gossip or criticism they received from other representatives of the Word made flesh. Or too familiar are the experiences of having few, if any, fellow Christians take a genuine interest in us by asking how we are and then really listening for a heartfelt answer. Indeed, how difficult James's words are to "take note of this: Everyone should be quick to listen, slow to speak and slow to become angry, for man's anger does not bring about the righteous life [of true community] that God desires" (1:19–20).

As simplistic as it sounds, filling our hearts with God's words and allowing them to fall from our lips toward others is often at the heart of a healthy community. And listening as Christ would—that is, with sincere compassion, grace, and kindness—then offers those around us a soothing balm for their wounds. Let us be careful to follow Paul's instruction in Ephesians 4:29: "Do not let any unwholesome talk come out of your mouths, but only what is helpful for building others up according to their needs, that it may benefit those who listen." If we exercised this practice of righteous communicating in our relationships with one another, the bride of Christ would be ready for her groom and the watching world would certainly want to celebrate in the wedding feast!

Peruse the Proverbs for passages about the power of words. Reflect on how these words, or others, have helped you on your Christian journey.

All in All

When we recognize that community is at the heart of our lives, our Lord's being, and our world's longings, why would we choose anything but its good? Of course, we will all fail, sin, and fall short of what God has called us to. Daily. That is all the more reason for us to speak grace and loving correction to one another, to communicate forgiveness and stability for one another, to offer kindness and hope in reminders of how deep and wide, high and long is the love of God. Because the fact remains, "If one part [of the body] suffers, every part suffers with it; if one part is honored, every part rejoices with it" (1 Cor. 12:26).

Medical research has concluded that a person's physical health is improved if he is willing to let go of bitterness,

unforgiveness, or pride. Our verbal expressions of forgiveness, pardon, and gentleness, then, not only foster personal
healing but spiritual wholeness and harmony for the whole
body of Christ. Likewise, our personal repentance does not
just set us free, but it brings corporate healing as well. True
repentance almost always is for the sake of Christ's body.
We don't come to Jesus in solitary confinement; we immediately enter into the family of God, his kingdom. The same
is true when we confess our sins, repenting of all unholi-
ness, because one part of the body affects the whole. We
are all in this together.

An incredible example of such Christian unity and reconciliation can be found in an event that occurred almost
sixty years ago. On a dark November day in 1940, Nazi war-
planes dropped enough bombs on Coventry, England, to
completely devastate the city's famous cathedral. Church
leaders and local Christians spent the night battling the
flames, praying for some act of God to intervene so they
might save their historic place of worship. But by morning, piles of brick and colored glass replaced the centuries-
old Anglican building; their miracle seemed elusive.

A few days later, one of the cathedral's reverends walked
slowly through the smoldering roof timbers and noticed several medieval nails. Then he made an extraordinary decision: Instead of becoming angry or despairing, he collected
the nails and wired them together to form a cross. As he
did, he became all the more convinced that the work of
God could not be so easily extinguished; with that, he sent
the small crosses to Christians in Germany as a symbol of
friendship. That day, the miracle of reconciliation—and
the International Centre for Christian Reconciliation—
was born at Coventry Cathedral. Today, the Cathedral's
International Centre for Christian Reconciliation partners
with Christians in seventy-five cities around the world and
conducts regular reconciliation services and conferences at

141

the cathedral as a continual reminder of the power of Christian unity.

The rector who sent those crosses understood the power and impact forgiveness would have on God's people and on the watching world, regardless of where they lived. As we come to the table of fellowship to eat together, our commitment to Christian community can be no less.

The prayer below is written on one of the remaining walls of Coventry Cathedral and is prayed each week by the congregation there. Consider its words, and pray it together with your spouse, family, or close Christian friends. Then ask God in silence to change your heart, transforming any bitterness into Christlike forgiveness.

Litany of Reconciliation

Leader: All have sinned and fallen short of the glory of God. The hatred which divides nation from nation, race from race, class from class,

People: Father forgive.

Leader: The covetous desires of people and nations to possess what is not their own,

People: Father forgive.

Leader: The greed which exploits the work of human hands and lays waste the earth,

142

People: Father forgive.

Leader: Our envy of the welfare and happiness of others,

People: Father forgive.

Leader: Our indifference to the plight of the imprisoned, the homeless, the refugee,

People: Father forgive.

Leader: The lust which dishonors the bodies of men, women, and children,

People: Father forgive.

Leader: The pride which leads us to trust in ourselves, and not in God,

People: Father forgive.

All: Be kind to one another, tender hearted, forgiving one another as God in Christ forgave you.

8

CONTEMPLATION:
SAVORING EACH MORSEL

The unexamined life is not worth living.
SOCRATES

A few years ago I had the opportunity to attend a conference celebrating the works of C. S. Lewis. Set in the shadows of centuries-old buildings and cathedrals, the Cambridge, England, university where Lewis once taught seemed an ideal place for such a gathering. People from all over the world and all walks of life came together for the two-week conference to discuss how the writings and ideas of this gifted apologist had radically altered their thinking and challenged their faith.

One night, as I strolled past the Cam River and into the most elegant dining hall I'd ever seen on a college campus, I noticed a young woman standing alone, waiting in line for dinner. After we exchanged introductions (she was a structural engineer from New Jersey), we began talking about how the lectures, workshops, and performances of the conference were affecting us. As I listened, I heard from her a story not at all unfamiliar to me: She had grown up in a suburban family who always went to church. She knew her family loved her and that her childhood congregation would provide her with spiritual guidance and emotional support whenever she needed either. Both "families" had shown the woman how to serve God and love others. But, she told me, she had often felt alienated or different because of her persistent questions and relentless curiosity. As a result, she always struggled with her intellect, questioning this or that, and wondered why her church frequently told her "just to accept things as they are." Yet, she felt she could never quite enter the Christian journey as long as she neglected developing her mind. Unfortunately, she was never encouraged to use her intellectual abilities in matters of faith.

"Only Lewis taught me how to do that," she said to me. "That's why I had to come here." When she first "met" Lewis in a book called *Mere Christianity,* it was as if she had finally found what she had always hoped for: a thoughtful, reflective Christian whose life and works gave her permission to ask questions and to use her brainy gifts for God's purposes.

As much as an active and balanced Christian life demands our commitment to solitude, service, and community, it is still not completely anchored without the final spiritual food group called contemplation. We can spend hours in prayer, serve at a local mission or church, and spend time building relationships in the body of Christ—like my friend

146

at the conference did—and still run the risk of leading what I call "a lopsided life." Just as three legs of a chair will never hold the weight of a person, merely incorporating community, service, and solitude into our lives will not completely "hold us up." We need the fourth leg of contemplation to keep us well supported and balanced, to keep us honest and real. Otherwise, it's too easy to stay isolated in these other areas and never do the hard work that thinking requires of us.

When we become contemplative, that is, when we really consider our ways, reflect on our motives, or ponder our purpose, we begin to display an integrity—or wholeness—of faith. That's why we must integrate the active practice of contemplation into our lives so we might become the people God has called us to be. In other words, we need to use our brains. And that requires nurturing an agile mind and developing a contemplative, reflective intellect that spurs us on to new places with our Maker. If we don't, our faith is reduced to stale, mundane, stagnant religion that does little good for anyone.

Write down what your personal definition of contemplation would be. What role has it played in your faith journey?

"Normal Equipment"

During the time in history that paved the way for the Enlightenment period, the French philosopher Descartes said, "I think, therefore, I am." He believed that the mere

147

act of an individual's thinking could shape his entire identity and behavior, needing little other than his own reasoning to create his destiny. Another Frenchman, Blaise Pascal, at around the same time, countered Descartes' now-famous statement with this Christian version: "I look for God; therefore, I have found him." Pascal's insight suggests that it is not our thinking alone that forms us. Rather it is our thoughtful search for God that shapes our identity and maps our destiny with him. Yet, before we dismiss one or the other entirely, let's consider how both men's proclamations are relevant in our study of contemplation.

It is certainly true that we "are what we think." Popular culture has long confirmed Descartes' truism, and multiple self-help books and seminars that offer effective principles for positive thinking or the like are obvious evidence. Though void of any reverence for the Almighty, such principles are often based on truths that *do* elicit positive change and call a person to rethink, or consider, the relation one's thought patterns have to one's lifestyle. In fact, counselors and health-care professionals who once referred to people with psychological problems as "emotionally disturbed" now are considering that it is the thinking patterns of these people—how they process, perceive, and interpret reality—that affect their physical, emotional, and behavioral well-being.

Long before Descartes or pop culture made this link between thinking and acting, though, the Bible explored the relation between a person's thoughts and actions. Proverbs 23:7 says that "as a man thinks within himself, so he is." The psalms are full of mandates to meditate, consider, and think on God's attributes so the believer's lifestyle will reflect a higher way. The disciples were challenged to be "of one mind" so their behavior would be consistently united, and the apostles Paul and Peter called on Christians to be transformed from the patterns of the world by "the renewing of your mind" and to "prepare your minds for action" (Rom. 12:2; 1 Peter 1:13). Of course, the greatest commandment even calls us to "love the Lord your God with all your . . . mind" (Matt. 22:37).

For the Christian, then, our thinking must be in the context of our relationship with the one who made our minds, the one who created order and balance from the beginning, who is wisdom and knowledge combined, who transcends time and experience, and who alone provides us with understanding and depths of insights beyond our own abilities. We must "look for God" and therefore, acknowledge, "I have found him." Why? So our thinking and our lives will reflect his. If we contemplate or study apart from him or for the mere intellectual act alone, we can anticipate chaos and meaninglessness coming at us like driftwood atop the ocean. Left to our own intellectual capacities, we fickle humans have a tendency to become miserable and double minded, chasing after any philosophy or idea that comes along. The apostle James even described such a person who engages in divided or double-minded thinking and praying as "a wave of the sea, blown and tossed by the wind." He went on to observe that such a man is "unstable in all he does" (1:6, 8).

So the call to a contemplative, or examined, life naturally invites the Creator's influence, the one who is "beyond our understanding," as Job 36:26 says. A simple word study helps us further clarify the active relationship between contemplation and the life our Maker desires: Contemplation is "the act of the mind in considering with attention; meditation; study; continued attention of the mind to a particular subject; it is keeping the idea, brought into the mind, sometimes actually in view. Holy meditation; attention to sacred things; a particular application of the foregoing definition. To have in contemplation, to intend or purpose, or to have under consideration." Synonyms include attentive, compare, consider, eye, heavenly, meditate, muse, practice, question, reflection, remember, retrospective,

149

wonder. Each part of this definition, as well as the synonyms, are positive and instructive for living an abundant life (though not necessarily an easy one). A thirteenth-century definition takes us deeper still: "concentration on spiritual things as a form of private devotion; a state of mystical awareness of God's being; an act of considering with attention; the act of regarding steadily; intention, expectation." All the words here—attention, wonder, consider, meditate, concentration, awareness—imply active, ongoing, and steady efforts to focus our minds on sacred things. Therefore, using our brains in relation to our faith—and in cooperation with our other three spiritual food groups—could only produce good fruit for God's kingdom.

We all know, however, that this is no easy task. Like my friend experienced, many U.S. Christians have viewed matters of the mind as potentially evil, dangerous, or threatening, thereby neglecting the development of their intellectual gifts. It is as if Proverbs 3:5–6, "Trust in the LORD with all your heart and lean not on your own understanding," has given Western Christians permission *not* to think or contemplate essential issues as they relate to our corporate lives with God. But, of course, this verse doesn't tell us to *ignore* our own understanding, just not to give it more place than it ought to have. It implies simply what we already know: The Lord is more trustworthy than our human understanding. But it never suggests our understanding is insignificant or unimportant.

Perhaps those who believe Christians ought not to think haven't looked hard enough at the biblical mandate to exercise our minds for God's sake. Others might have perceived the mind as an unreliable, unredeemed part of our being and have therefore been taught to blindly accept their faith without ever questioning it. Perhaps it is precisely as the Trappist monk Thomas Merton described in his early essay *What Is Contemplation?*:

Why do we think of the gift of contemplation . . . as something essentially strange and esoteric reserved for a small class of almost unnatural beings and prohibited to everyone else? It is perhaps because we have forgotten that contemplation is the work of the Holy Spirit acting on our souls through His gifts of Wisdom and Understanding with special intensity to increase and perfect our love for Him. These gifts are part of the normal equipment of Christian sanctity. They are given to us at Baptism, and if they are given it is presumably because God wants them to be developed. . . . But it is also true that God often measures His gifts by our desire to receive them, and by our cooperation with His grace, and the Holy Spirit will not waste any of His gifts on people who have little or no interest in them.[1]

Obviously, ignoring the gift of contemplation has only produced shallow, ineffective witnesses in our current age who cannot adequately defend the faith of some of history's greatest thinkers. By so doing, it has also perpetuated an image to the unbelieving world that American Christians are often dogmatic, isolated, judgmental, and essentially unable to engage in discussions with those who think differently than we do. Maybe we as Americans are afraid of difference, mystery, or questions. Given our American-dream mind-set, it seems we'd much rather have control, answers, and comfortableness than risk entering into the spiritual arena of uncertainty and exploration. It is unfortunate that many of us haven't yet embraced what contemporary Christian poet Luci Shaw recognized: "The known is enriched when you move into the unknown. Mystery enhances, questions don't need be answered to nurture the imagination."[2]

Christians, then, need to use our brains and explore mystery, questions, reflection, all of which help us contemplate the truth of the gospel. When we do, our solitary fellowship is deepened, our service is lightened, and our community becomes more meaningful. We are also better equipped to articulate and defend the Good News to a world in which skewed thinking seems normal, a world that confuses love with sex, power with corruption, wealth with happiness, and enjoyment with amusement. (Even the word *amusement* gives us insight into our modern culture's shallow state: Muse is the thought, mind, or inspiration behind some creative act or person. Anytime an *a* is placed before a word, it indicates a negative connotation or nullifies the meaning of the word. So a-muse-ment literally means, not with thought, mindless, and uninspiring!)

Yet, we also must be clear about what contemplation is *not:* It is not merely acquiring more information, Christian or otherwise. We have enough already, especially in the contemporary religious marketplace. This multibillion-dollar industry has produced many, many books: books that teach us how to pray, how to be a better parent, how to be single and content; books that teach us what's wrong with America, what's wrong with the government, what's wrong with the church; books that teach us why small groups are important, why communication is essential, why God allows good things to happen to bad people. In fact, we have more Christian information than at any other time in history. And it's available online or in paperback, hardback, bumper stickers, CDs, videos, audios, T-shirts, or magazines. We have more access to solid biblical principles, to sound doctrines, to safe theology than ever before. Like the rest of the country, we in Christendom are on information overload.

I know a middle-aged woman who grew up in a strong Christian home. Most of her adult life has been spent reading Christian books, attending church, and singing in the choir. She is a faithful volunteer with the Sunday school children and a regular participant in the women's Bible study. Often, she will loan friends and neighbors the latest religious book she's reading. "This will change your life," she tells them, as she rattles off other book titles and CDs featured on that week's Christian best-seller list. The shelves in her apartment are packed with popular Christian novels and teaching books. Meanwhile, she has struggled for years with what her life's purpose is, with understanding who she is in Christ and how much he cherishes her. Because she is single, she believes only a man's love will truly fulfill her; consequently, time and again she's found herself in an abusive sexual relationship with a man who's told her he was a Christian. Somehow, all the study, all the books and Bible studies, all the Christian data in the world has not changed her deep insecurity. Often, she complains to me how "stuck" she feels in her life. Why? Because information does not always lead to insight. The mere acquisition of it does not guarantee change.

In fact, sometimes I wonder how much good all this Christian information is doing across the country. In the past forty years as this industry has profited and grown for "religion's sake," so, too, has our nation seen an increase in social problems. Homelessness, domestic violence, teen suicides, divorce, racism, poverty, and immorality have risen to sad proportions, and I hardly believe another Christian book will make a dent in addressing these troubles. Don't get me wrong: I am grateful for the many books and Christian writers whose messages have personally challenged me to a deeper spiritual walk. I wonder, though, what our country might look like had the millions of dollars spent on Christian stuff instead been channeled into urban ministries, health centers, or youth arts and recreation programs. I wonder, too, about women like my friend; what if they had spent less time and energy accumulating Christian information and more time thoughtfully reflecting or meditating on God's promises? Obviously, more information does not (in and of itself) promote positive change, and it is not contemplation.

Nor is contemplation similar to the secular pursuit of intellectualism that often struts its smarts like a peacock does his

153

feathers. Sometimes, degrees, honors, academic seminars, and dissertations foster false exteriors of authority and lofty qualifications; as a result, we now have more "experts" in more fields doing more obscure studies on irrelevant areas than at any other time. Millions of dollars have been spent in the name of research through academic institutions, foundations, and government agencies with the hope that we could become a more progressive society and retain our world prominence. Yet, none have come close to eradicating poverty, sicknesses, injustices, or oppression. (Even Christian conferences and seminars throw hours and hours of lectures and teachings at attendees, with little time for participants to reflect on or ponder the content as they're hurried off to the next workshop.) No, the appropriation of academic knowledge and study is not the cure-all to society's ills or the proverbial fountain of youth. Nor is it contemplation either.

Instead, true biblical contemplation moves beyond information to insight, beyond knowledge and degrees to the wisdom of application and change. It is normal equipment for the normal Christian who desires to live a balanced life.

Reflect for a few moments on Proverbs 4:5–9. Why do you think wisdom is both supreme and costly?

Thinking Time

If contemplation, or the active exercise of our minds, is to be a normal attribute of the Christian walk, then we must schedule time for it in a variety of means. (We'll talk more about the many forms of contemplation in the next chapter.) Yet, too often the demands of ordinary life—meetings, car pools, chores, projects, or gatherings—keep us from sitting down with a good book, studying the Bible, or opening our journal to think through some hard issues by writing. Contemplation, then, automatically implies leaving the busyness of our lives for the sake of reflecting on its purpose. Lest we be consumed by appointments and schedules, we must view contemplative time as essential for our personal growth, which then naturally affects our relationships with others. Notice how the psalmist continually calls us to meditate on God's wonders, to remember his works, and to consider our ways. Jesus' constant use of parables, hard sayings, and sermons challenged his listeners to think deeply about the truth of his message. So it is never a waste of time to reflect on the way, the truth, and the life (John 14:6) insofar as it pushes us deeper into a relationship with our Creator and spills over into all that we do. Even Paul prayed for the church at Philippi that their "love may abound more and more in *knowledge* and *depth of insight*, so that you may be able to discern what is best and may be pure and blameless until the day of Christ, filled with the fruit of righteousness that comes through Jesus Christ—to the glory and praise of God" (1:9–11, emphasis mine).

In other words, contemplation, or thinking time, gives us new ways to see the world, new prayers to pray for others (like Phil. 1:9–11), new understandings about Scripture passages we may have read several times before, and new insights to lead us closer to the person God always dreamed we would be. I like how one Catholic leader put it: "Every man needs contemplation; it fulfills the deep need to seize the unity of the divine and the human." In its simplest terms, contemplative time away from the busy demands of life teaches us to pay better attention to it when we return.

Above all, though, contemplation is consistent reflection, attention, and meditation—"love abounding in knowledge and depth of insight"—that has a very specific purpose: changing us more and more into God's image and filling us "with the fruit of righteousness that comes through Jesus Christ." We must not view it merely as an intellectual exercise but rather a tool that the Almighty uses to chisel away at his masterpiece, to create a work of art that is free and loved and whole—"to the glory and praise of God." A painting never gets painted by the artist who only talks about his art. The patient, consistent act of choosing colors combined with careful, thoughtful strokes is what creates a fine picture. It is an ongoing process that yields beautiful rewards.

So it is with contemplating truth and exercising our minds. A great harvest will eventually be reaped as a result of taking the time to train our intellects in submission to the King of Kings. That's exactly what happened to a guy named Daniel and his three friends, Shadrach, Meshach, and Abednego. They were young men, handsome and strong, but not really certain what they were supposed to do with their lives until an unusual job opportunity came along. Because their parents had raised them well, they were willing to do just about anything; they were quick learners and hard workers. So when they heard that the king in their town was looking for a few good men, they decided to apply and soon found themselves learning the "language and literature" of the locals. For the next three years, they committed themselves to studying and being trained in the king's service, careful to honor the God of their youth with every aspect of their lives, including their physical and mental diet.

God likes that kind of focused willingness, so much so that the Bible says, "To these four young men God gave knowledge and understanding of all kinds of literature and learning. And Daniel could understand visions and dreams of all kinds" (Dan. 1:17). The benefits of appropriating God's gifts quickly came. When the king talked with them, he found none equal to Daniel and his friends: "So they entered the king's service. In every matter of wisdom and understanding about which the king questioned them, he found them ten times better than all the magicians and enchanters in his whole kingdom" (Dan. 1:19–20). Daniel and his pals earned great status along with the king's favor because they knew that their minds were a gift from God to be used and exercised for his honor and purposes.

If ever there was a good example of the fruit of a man's intellectual labor, we can find it in Daniel and company. These four young men did not wince when it came to tackling the languages and literature of the cultures, to acquiring knowledge for the sake of their newly assigned roles. But they also did not compromise their faith in the midst of heady competition and mind games. Of course, their colleagues were not happy at the foursome's rising status; nonetheless, God continued to honor their efforts, rescue them from the schemes of their jealous enemies, and increase their blessings because of their determination to become holy thinkers.

The apostle Paul must have been equally inspired. When he was in Athens waiting for some fellow workers, "he was greatly distressed to see that the city was full of idols" (Acts 17:16). But, like Daniel, he also did not retreat from the ideological differences that confronted him; instead, he "reasoned in the synagogue" and even used some of the works of local poets and the words of religious scribes in his own evangelistic message: "For in him [God] we live and move and have our being. As some of your own poets have said, 'We are his offspring.' Therefore since we are God's offspring, we should not think that the divine being is like gold or silver or stone—an image made by man's design and skill. In the past God overlooked such ignorance, but now he commands all people everywhere to repent" (Acts 17:28–30). As a result, "a few men became followers of Paul and believed" (Acts 17:34). Paul's famous Mars Hill sermon reminds us again of the strategic purposes God has for us—and others—when we are willing to do our homework and use our brains.

Read through Paul's sermon in Acts 17. What else does it teach you about how we are to use our minds?

Truth That Tells

I'm told that secret agents often used to study real U.S. dollar bills, memorizing every letter, stroke, and colored shadow on the original so that when they would see a counterfeit dollar, they would immediately recognize the difference. That's how our contemplative life should be: We should be so saturated in the truth of God's message that anything counter becomes obvious. Daniel and Paul showed us that process well. We can do no less if we are to live effective balanced lives for Christ. This automatically implies that we are careful with what we hear and see, with what we feed our minds since we know it will eventually bear fruit in our lifestyles.

For example, consider how our culture has latched onto the old biblical adage that "the truth will set you free." We like how it sounds and how it feels knowing that truth will bring such an ear-tickling security as freedom. It is a pithy, sugarcoated presentation of what we all yearn for, yet it is incomplete. From movie scripts and comedians' remarks to editorial pages, it is interesting how flippantly we hear that "the truth will set you free," relegating it to the ever popular category of instant gratification. What's missing, though, is a thoughtful consideration of the cost of getting there. When we really think about it we recognize that the truth alone does not instantly set us free, nor does it give us such a sentimental feeling. That is what I call truth without backbone. We need only consider how a careless—but true—remark to a friend about his irritating manners or to a co-worker about her inability to do the job will fall on their ears. These impulsive truths do not set people free in such situations; instead, they pierce, hurt, and sting, often producing an oppressive bitterness or lasting mistrust.

Arthur Miller's tragic play *Death of a Salesman* reveals how the discovery of truth can harm and hurt even the deepest relationships. It is the sad story of Willy Loman, an old salesman whose time is about up. Willy's two sons have grown up admiring their dad, wanting to be like him in every way, idolizing him, and trying desperately to please him. What they never saw, though, was that their father lived a life of lies; he was never a great salesman, though he told his sons he was. He was never a popular man, though he made his sons believe he had many friends. Because Willy never recognizes the reality of his own shortcomings, he remains trapped in his own denial and deception while trying hard to maintain an image of strength and dignity. So when his oldest son, Biff, learns the truth of his father's extramarital affair, he is devastated. The secret is out—Willy is a failure. Biff wonders if his father has ever been honest with him and plummets into deep despair, emotional bondage, and disappointment over the knowledge of his father's true character. Because Willy can never admit the truth of his wrongdoing, nothing is able to restore their relationship. Both father and son are shattered by Willy's sin because Biff sees the ugly truth that his father will never embrace.

The moral of the story? Instant truth shocks and hurts. It destroys trust and kills perspective, like it did Biff's. Persevering truth, however, heals and frees—it is relational, ongoing, and life producing, the very stuff of contemplation. That's why the old adage must be looked at in its proper context. In John 8:31–32, Jesus is speaking to the Jewish leaders about how to determine if they are really Abraham's descendants, if they are true followers of God: "To the Jews who had believed him, Jesus said, 'If you hold to my teaching, you are really my disciples. Then you will know the truth, and the truth will set you free.'" Some translations read, "If you continue in my word . . ." Obviously, the "if . . . then" mandate changes our contemporary view of truth setting us free. The charge Jesus makes includes a persistent, steadfast holding or study of his teaching; only this persevering truth will bring us the freedom we yearn for. And only this is true contemplation: consistent time set apart to know intimately the teachings of Christ, to meditate on his truth and life, to hide God's Word in our hearts, and to reflect on his laws and statures. It is exactly as Richard J. Foster described in his popular book *Celebration of Discipline*:

> Many Christians remain in bondage to fears and anxieties simply because they do not avail themselves of the Discipline of study. They may be faithful in church attendance and earnest in fulfilling their religious duties and still they are not changed. . . . They may sing with gusto; pray in the Spirit, live as obediently as they know, even receive divine visions and revelations; and yet the tenor of their lives remains unchanged. Why? Because they have never taken up one of the central ways God uses to change us: study.

Jesus made it unmistakably clear that it is the knowledge
of the truth that will set us free.[3]

Because Jesus teaches us to see everything in the light
of his truth and compassion toward others, we must enter
the sometimes difficult, sometimes frightening world of the
mind so that our actions reflect his. Early desert fathers,
mystics, or monks who entered what they called "the contemplative life" did so with the conviction that their continual reflection would provide a feast of understanding,
an assurance that could not be penetrated by outside distractions, a security that would sustain them throughout
their holy and centered lives. Indeed, it is true for all of us
that such meditation on God's ways and purposes will bring
ours into cooperation with his.

Obviously, then, the seeds we plant in our minds will
produce either chaos or peace, disorder or balance. That's
why the Christian must heed the apostle's words in Philippians 4:8: "Finally, brothers, whatever is true, whatever is
noble, whatever is right, whatever is pure, whatever is
lovely, whatever is admirable—if anything is excellent or
praiseworthy—think about such things." When we think
on that which is true, noble, right, pure, and lovely, we are
thinking about heaven, reflecting it in our lives, and enjoying peace during this earthly time.

I learned this (for the hundredth time!) while I was writing this chapter. As the saying goes, "life happened" as I
was preparing for this section of the book: The community
of Christian friends I live with had to move out of one house
in hopes of moving into another that wasn't quite finished
being renovated. That meant we put our belongings in stor-
age while we relied on the mercy of other friends to host
us until our new home was completed. Meanwhile, my car
broke down, a good friend was diagnosed with leukemia,
another's brother-in-law was killed in a motorcycle accident, and I wasn't quite sure how I was going to make it

through. The difficult circumstances quickly distracted me—as they often do—from that which is true, noble, right, and pure.

But writing this chapter helped me remember I was faced with a choice: I could yield to the challenges and remain stressed and miserable (and contaminate everyone around me with the same). At first, of course, I did whine through a good amount of self-pity. The only problem was the pity party turned out to be exhausting and depleting. My energy was zapped and I was hurting others in the process. My other option was to recall the wonders God had so faithfully performed in my life in the past. Surely, he had not changed. Surely, he would not leave me nor forsake me. Surely, he was bigger than my whining and pity.

He was. And is.

Then one morning in the midst of the challenges, I began wrestling (as usual) with God, challenging him on what was happening and making sure he heard my complaints. When I'd finally had my fill, my mind surprisingly "called up" two verses I memorized years ago, like a computer calls up an old file: "Let us fix our eyes on Jesus, the author and perfecter of our faith, who for the joy set before him endured the cross, scorning its shame, and sat down at the right hand of the throne of God. *Consider* him who endured such opposition from sinful men, so that you will not grow weary and lose heart" (Heb. 12:2–3, emphasis mine). I was struck and stilled at the same time. My fists relaxed. The quiet surrounded me like a cool breeze on a hot humid day, and I literally couldn't move.

"Consider him who endured such opposition from sinful men, *so that* you will not grow weary and lose heart." Over and over, my mind considered the life of Christ, the opposition he endured, the suffering he experienced, the pain he felt. I thought of him with the Pharisees, in the crowds of people demanding his help, in the Garden of Gethsemane

162

praying to his Father, and finally on the cross, bleeding, alone, agonizing. My attitude was changing.

"Who for the joy set before him endured the cross . . ." Now, a strange thing was happening: My heart was singing a hymn, and my mouth was whispering a thankful prayer of confession. I felt lighter, focused, refreshed, while anxiety and stress became unwelcomed visitors in an already crowded room. I sat still, grateful, open. I did not realize how hungry for heaven I had been until I savored these morsels of truth.

I don't know how long I stayed with God that morning; I do know that considering Jesus through God's Word renewed my mind, which changed my attitude, which gave me more energy to accomplish what he had given me to do and to encourage others along the way. In short, this simple act of contemplation helped me regain my footing and restore my balance in a potentially trying time. God's truth anchored me again.

And, thankfully, it will continue to do so in a variety of forms.

Ask God right now to renew your mind
and to help you focus on that which is
true, noble, right, pure, and lovely.
Receive the stillness and presence
of his peace as you do.

9

CONTEMPLATION:
TASTE, SMELL, ENJOY

One should listen to a little song, read a good poem, or look at a fine painting every single day. And if possible, say something sensible about it.

JOHANN WOLFGANG VON GOETHE,
THE "POETRY IN MOTION" SERIES
ON A NEW YORK CITY SUBWAY

To enjoy the unending feast of life with Christ, to be unmovable in our faith, is a sweet invitation to the adventure of contemplation. We consider our ways, like the psalmist wrote in Psalm 119:59; we meditate on his wonders (119:27); we remember the deeds of the Lord (77:11) and enter his words, which give light and understanding to the simple (119:130), hiding them in our hearts that we might not sin against him (119:11). In each of these acts, we still our hearts and focus our minds in the moment, entering the realm of the imagination for the sake of heaven. We are literally *mindful* of God's presence.

Such daily reflection in what we call quiet times (or devotions) is perhaps the most common form of contemplation we experience. Indeed, it is crucial for maintaining our balance and ensuring our growth. But have we considered the numerous other ways we can feed our minds, strengthen our faculties, increase our spiritual wisdom, and transform ourselves into the image of Christ? Contrary to what some might believe, God's truth as it relates to the human experience is not easily packaged nor contained. Obviously, it is not *only* available in sermons, Bible studies, or Christian books, though, of course, each of these forms of teaching can be a primary method that the Maker uses to change our thinking and renew our minds. Yet, if we explore the arts and literature, discussions and writing, even nature and serene settings, we'll also encounter delightful and challenging avenues for building a contemplative lifestyle.

Hell: A Bookless World

Though the Scriptures describe hell as a fiery place separated from our loving God, my nontheological idea of hell (on earth) is a world separated from books. I can't imagine what life would have been like for me as a child growing up without Nancy Drew mysteries or Little House on the Prairie books. Some of my first role models came into my life through books: abolitionist Frederick Douglass, Olympic athlete Babe

Didrikson Zaharias, and Appalachian missionary Christy Huddleston. Their stories taught me about tenacity, courage, and commitment, character traits I have always admired in others and hoped for in my own life. In fact, their influence led me to a book that affected my thinking and living more than any other, a book that has been a best-seller many times over, transcending cultures and times and geography, surviving wars and laws that condemned it: the Holy Bible.

Christians are people of *the* Book, an anthology comprised of many genres of writing: Prose, drama, poetry, narratives, parables, sermons, letters, you name it, all make up the wonderful book we know as God's Word. Such an identity with the Word made flesh (John 1:1) ought to make us appreciate the gift of language and story in other books as well. Why? Because the world of literature—from stories and poetry to novels and plays—has an unusual ability to take readers into another's experience and shape their lives in unique, exciting, and sometimes startling ways. In their word pictures, we see a new wisdom. In their changing characters, we understand humanity a bit more. On journeys we never imagined possible, we become their companions and students. As C. S. Lewis said, "We read to know we're not alone."

What are some of your favorite childhood books? What did you appreciate about them?

Life, then, without books would be a dreary and frightening thing, making the contemplative life impossible and the balanced life, well, lopsided. That is precisely what contemporary North American author Ray Bradbury thought when he wrote his now-classic book, *Fahrenheit 451*. First published in 1950 (long before interactive television or personal computers changed the world), *Fahrenheit* was the first science fiction book I ever encountered, and I wasn't quite sure what I was getting into when I opened it. But like an amusement park mirror, it distorted my reality just enough to make me really appreciate its important message and story: Guy Montag, an emotionally vacant fireman, lives in a technologically induced society that has long found books obsolete, threatening even, so much so that people are robotic and lifeless, and the fireman's job is not to put out fires but to start them, using pages and words as kindling! However, the lettered flames, along with an early encounter with a distinctly poetic young woman named Clarisse, begin to capture Guy's curiosity about the power of these books he's been burning, inviting him out of the techno-drugged hell and into the dangerous task of . . . living.

He begins to question authority, hide books in his apartment, and, consequently, dives into a relentless quest for truth. When he secretly meets up with an old English professor whose memory is a delicious library of Homer, the Bible, Shakespeare, and Shaw, Montag hands the professor a book he has stolen, and the starved fireman's meal begins:

> Do you know why books such as this are so important? [says professor Fabor]. Because they have quality. And what does the word quality mean? To me it means texture. This book has pores. It has features. This book can go under the microscope. *You'd find life under the glass*, streaming past in infinite profusion. The more pores, the more truthfully recorded details of life per square inch you can get on a sheet of paper, the more "literary" you are. That's my definition anyway. Telling detail. Fresh detail. The good writers touch life often. The mediocre ones run a quick hand over her. The bad ones rape her and leave her for the flies. So now do you see why books are hated and feared? They show the pores in the face of life. [But] the comfortable people want only wax moon faces, poreless, hairless, expressionless (emphasis mine).[1]

The morsels are just tasty enough for Montag to risk his status by sneaking more books before he torches the piles. Of course, he is found out and the chase begins: Montag fights for a life he never thought—literally—possible, while the powers-that-be battle to preserve their bookless, and therefore, mindless, society, intent on destroying anyone who might disrupt the "comfortable people." Yet Montag is more alive than he ever has been, escapes the evil foes, and surfaces safely on the old train tracks outside the city with other banished literati—professors, writers, philosophers, and the like. Their word-centered community symbolizes the unending influence and vitality of stories and language. With them, books never die: They're hidden in their memories and savored at every meal.

Bradbury's novel has been perceived as prophetic and essential for battling the intrusion that can come from censorship and technology. True enough. But it is much more than that. *Fahrenheit* to me is a spiritual challenge about the stuff of living: to pay attention to the sound of a friend's voice, the smell of a favorite meal, the colors of a sun-splashed shore. Words give them meaning, heaven on earth if you will, and the book's bookless world is really a lesson in priorities, showing us the difference between the abundant life an active mind brings and the numbing existence of a mindless one.

But lest we think this bookless world exists only in science fiction, we need to remember how history itself confirms Bradbury's warnings. Whenever a corrupt king or queen, for example, rose to power throughout Europe's Middle Ages, reading was proclaimed illegal or made inaccessible for the poor or working class and reserved only for wealthy citizens and court officials. Peasants were not allowed to read, nor could they afford the expense of books or tutoring, and if they were taught religion at all, it was through the use of stained glass windows in churches or cathedrals. When Gutenberg invented the printing press, he did so with the express purpose of producing copies of the Bible for the masses of people who before had been oppressed because of their illiteracy.

Documented in our own country's legal records are shameful laws that prohibited African slaves from ever learning to read or write, or white people from even teaching them. The reason? They could become "dangerous or unruly" if they learned to read. And of course, during this century, we've watched from afar how some oppressive governments in other countries have treated the works of certain authors and playwrights, banning their books and sending the writers to prison. Yet, during these same times, well-intentioned parents in our own country have publicly denied access to particular books in libraries and schools because they believe their children will be wrongly influenced.

Obviously, many have recognized how powerful a tool literature can be in shaping the values and imagination of a person. For the Christian, then, reading all types of literary works has special significance, leading us to the intriguing place where divine and human meet, where emotional and spiritual intersect. When we view a good play, listen to a poem read out loud, or turn the pages of a classic novel, we can't help but be moved. Why? Because we have nurtured a solitary fellowship with the creative God, been changed by the greatest story of all time, and so cannot help but appreciate the stories and words of others that give us a glimpse both of common suffering and divine grace. I love how John Murray described it in his essay "The Solace of Words: Literature and Suffering":

> In nearly every life, there comes a moment when a person must face the ultimate injustices and indignities alone. A work of literature at that time can relieve a pain no amount of morphine can numb, can answer those questions that will forever confound science, can restore a faith no sur-

geon, however skilled, could transplant. We cannot endure suffering without books for long.[2]

Indeed, the tool of literature encourages our battered souls and helps guide us through the ongoing tension of living creatively on this earth while preparing for the eternal. In stories, we are confronted with the evidence of a fallen world, the challenges of a broken, glorious humanity, yet reminded of heaven's participation in bringing about redemption on earth.

So when we set our minds on things above (Col. 3:2), when we "put on the new self, which is being renewed in knowledge in the image of its Creator" (Col. 3:10), we can learn from literature about living abundantly on earth and enjoying our Maker in the midst of it. We are both in this world but not of it, thereby recognizing stories and beauty as God-inspired, heavenly instruments that call us upward. In other words, as the kingdom of God is a place of beauty and hope, and as the Old Testament is filled with descriptions of heavenly attributes when describing the holy temple, so, too, should we view creativity and art as reflections of our Creator, one who did not just make the heavens but the earth as well, splashing it with brilliant colors, incredible shapes, and intricate designs. God's very act of creation in both nature and humans is cause to celebrate the arts!

Consider the powerful experience of visiting the theater and witnessing the corporate miracle that can happen when actors, musicians, playwrights, directors, and technicians work together to tell a story on stage. Or the moving effect a painting of the crucifixion or a photograph of a smiling child can have on the viewer, causing him to consider a new perspective of an old message. Or listening to a song or a symphony in which the music reaches an inexpressible, almost magical point, piercing through our intellect to teach us more than a sermon or lecture ever could.

How many times have we sung a hymn or heard a harmonious choir and been reminded of something greater? As one critic wrote when he first listened to *A Sonata for Piano* by Beethoven, the tranquil first movement immediately created in his mind images of moonlight on the waves!

Even reading poetry specifically can help connect us to both human and divine qualities we too easily overlook, challenging us to continue nurturing the art of reflection and stirring in us some heartfelt response to something greater than ourselves. Wheaton College professor Leland Ryken explained such a process in his book *The Liberated Imagination*:

> The need to unpackage the meaning of individual words and images makes reading poetry a meditative or contemplative act in a way that reading a story is not. Poetry requires slow reading, in contrast to the faster pace of narrative. Instead of hurrying to find out what happens next, we must, as we read Psalm 23 for instance, stop to consider what kinds of human provision are embodied in such metamorphic pictures as sheep resting in green pastures beside still waters or being led on safe ("right") paths.[3]

Indeed, poetry makes us stop, think, and imagine something our minds before hadn't explored. I know of someone who considered Christ's love for the first time in her busy life when she heard the poetry of a Christian friend of mine during a reading at a coffeehouse in Greenwich Village!

Schedule into your calendar an artistic event this week, a concert, art exhibit, play, or poetry reading. As you experience it, consider what it shows you about truth.

Discriminating Palates

In spite of all the great places literature can take us, we must not forget that the mind is easily swayed and influenced; therefore, contemplation requires that we are careful and thoughtful with what we feed it. Why else would the apostle Paul have told the Corinthian church, "I am afraid that just as Eve was deceived by the serpent's cunning, your minds may somehow be led astray from your sincere and pure devotion to Christ" (2 Cor. 11:3)? He knew that if we don't work diligently on directing our minds toward the bright morning star, we can easily float off course. It is therefore essential that we develop another art and tool for living a balanced life: discernment.

I was curious how our high-tech Internet age would define discernment, so I did an online search: Discernment is "the power or faculty of the mind by which it distinguishes one thing from another; power of viewing differences in objects, and their relations and tendencies; penetrative and discriminate mental vision. Discernment is keenness and accuracy of mental vision; penetration is the power of seeing deeply into a subject in spite of everything that intercepts the view; discrimination is a capacity of tracing out minute distinctions and the nicest shades of thought. A discerning man is not easily misled; one of a penetrating mind sees a multitude of things which escape others; a discriminating judgment detects the slightest differences." (With an incredible variety of information and web sites so easily accessible, we can only hope that one will have the "capacity of tracing out minute distinctions" as well as "discriminating judgment" when surfing the Net!)

From Webster's Revised Unabridged Dictionary, discernment means "to see or understand the difference; to make distinction; as, to discern between good and evil, truth and falsehood." The relationship discernment has, then, to contemplation (and therefore, to balance) is critical; it is not enough for the Christian merely to be reflective in his encounter with the arts or a Bible study. If it does not help sharpen our mental vision, teaching us to distinguish and discriminate good from evil, truth from falsehood, giving us "a penetrating mind" that "detects the slightest differences," we will be "easily misled." As we've already discussed, so much stimuli and information bombard us daily that if we don't develop a discriminating mental palate, we will drown in a sea of intellectual choices and hollow philosophies.

To determine how to be contemplative in the arts, to select a film or video, for instance, we must be discerning or we run the risk of feeding our brains with food that only clogs our spiritual arteries. We must learn to make distinctions between art that is honest and excellent and art that does not necessarily reflect a good God. Remember Paul's charge to the Philippian church? "And this is my prayer: that your love may abound more and more in knowledge and depth of insight, *so that you may be able to discern* what is best and may be pure and blameless until the day of Christ" (1:9–10, emphasis mine). Discernment comes when our knowledge and depth of insight increase in direct proportion to our solitude, community, and service. Indeed, it is in love for God and others that we develop a "keenness and accuracy" of spiritual vision. As a result of time spent (either alone or with others) in interactive, contemplative prayer with the King of Kings, listening to his words, considering his truth, remembering his standards for artistic beauty, reflecting on his call to think on that which is lovely, good, and praiseworthy, we are kept "pure and blameless."

In his essay "What's a Good Story?" Walter Wangerin Jr. addressed this distinction in a most helpful way:

There are two standards by which to judge the value of literature, movies, television, songs, art—failing either one of which, they fail to be wholly good: the form and the sub-

174

stance. Sound and sense. Art must obey the best techni-
cal conventions of its craft, and it must obey truth. It must
love beauty, and it must love truth. The truth of the finest
art, though it decry the sin in us with accurate depictions,
must also cry us upward, call us into relationship with God,
revise the "reality" we once had believed in—and do all
with craft as crafty as the Creator's.[4]

Proverbs 22:29 says, "Do you see a man skilled in his
work? He will serve before kings; he will not serve before
obscure men." Such practical wisdom calls artists who are
Christians to excellence in their crafts and contemplatives
to discern and acknowledge such skill. There is no place
for mediocrity in God's kingdom; our standards of commitment, respect, and grace must be evident to all in how
we interact with aesthetics, art, and pop culture. We ought
not settle for less.

A great example of this is the Catholic Southern writer
Flannery O'Connor. During her short writing career from
1950 to 1964 (when she died of lupus at age thirty-nine),
O'Connor took seriously her call to the vocation of writing; she read history's best writers, studied at some of the
most reputable writing programs, attended mass every
morning, scrupulously observed the culture in which she
lived, and constantly revised her work. When a journalist
once asked her why she wrote, she responded simply,
"Because I am good at it." Her comment did not come from
an arrogant heart but rather a humble and certain acknowledgment of her calling and commitment as a writer.

That is no doubt why her works are read today in public high school and university English classes. She is considered by many nonreligious writers, scholars, and critics
to be one of America's most gifted fiction writers of this
century. O'Connor was "skilled in her work and so served
before kings." Yet, I believe the most exciting aspect of
her legacy is that once people are drawn to her fine writ-

ing, they must also confront her Christian beliefs. Why? Because you cannot read a Flannery O'Connor short story without getting a clear picture of her theology. Each story brilliantly (though often violently) shows man's depravity and his incredible need for God's grace. Of course in doing so, the reader becomes quite uncomfortable with the reality she presents. There is no eye-tickling here; truth slaps hard, yet humorously, in her stories. (I even know of one college professor who had to teach an O'Connor story in an American literature course one semester. While studying the terrible hypocrisy of the main character, he so identified that he fell on his knees and converted to Christianity!)

O'Connor's masterful use of language earned her the right to be read by an unbelieving culture. As a result, she had an inevitable opportunity to proclaim the message of Christ's truth. She did this because she dared to show writing that was original yet universal: full of real human life and redemption, sorrow and triumph, good and evil. As O'Connor said in her insightful nonfiction work *Mystery and Manners*,

> The novelist tries to give you, within the form of the book, a total experience of human nature at any time. For this reason the greatest dramas naturally involve the salvation or loss of the soul. Where there is no belief in the soul, there is very little drama. The Christian novelist is distinguished from his pagan colleagues by recognizing sin as sin. According to his heritage he sees it not as sickness or an accident of environment, but as a responsible choice of offense against God which involves his eternal future. Either one is serious about salvation or one is not.[5]

If ever one modeled discernment in her approach to her culture, her craft, and her Christian faith, it was Flannery O'Connor. And there's no question one needs the ability of discernment when reading one of her stories, an adventure that often takes us to the very core of what sits on the throne of our hearts. Our sinful nature usually and gleefully crowns self (and all its concerns) as king on that throne. We pursue our own comfort or careers, whims and wishes, and as a result, often choose entertainment (or amusement) that feeds our selfish fancies. We want art (or books or videos) that builds *us* up, rather than pointing us upward. It is exactly as O'Connor said, "What people don't realize is how much religion costs. They think faith is a big electric blanket, when of course it is the cross."[6]

Consequently, when authentic biblical discernment comes into the contemplative picture, our true idols are revealed, and our hearts are called to repentance. In other words, art, or any creative form, can never receive more importance or devotion, given more power or worship, than the Creator himself. Art—aesthetics, movies, dance, theater, or literature—finds its rightful place when it serves only as an instrument the Maker uses to shape and color our lives. It is not the object of our worship but rather the vehicle that leads us to enjoy the Worshiped One in the now. Though it requires the discipline of discernment, its rewards offer a life that is fully lived in union with the Prince of Peace.

Recite a favorite psalm out loud, slowly.
Listen to its poetry.
What images does it create in your mind?
What does it remind you about God?

177

Creative Options

As art, books, discernment, creativity, and Bible study offer important ingredients to the contemplative feast, so, too, are there a variety of other nourishing foods that we need for feeding our minds. When Joshua led the Israelites (in Joshua 3) across the dry land of the Jordan River, he sent back twelve appointed men to retrieve what he called memorial stones. Those stones were to remind the people that nothing was too difficult for God, not even parting the water. An active memory, then, is essential for keeping our faith anchored in the person of Jesus Christ.

I've often imagined what it must have been like for Joshua and his motley crew to approach that flowing river. God had promised to be with them, to protect and guide them, yet their limited human vision saw a strong current of water in front of them. Deep, overpowering water. Smack in front of them. They must have eyed each other suspiciously, wondering what kind of joke this was. Still, one decided to stick a toe in. And, amazingly, another followed. Soon, the whole bunch of complaining souls was crossing the river on *dry* ground, looking at piles and heaps of water on either side of them. It must have been either a deafeningly quiet scene or one of mass hysteria. Who could believe that such a strong river would stop, stand straight up, and then create a dry path through to the other side?! Yes, those who see the wonder of God *must* believe. And they must remember.

Yet, it is also not difficult to imagine why Joshua sent his men back for the stones; how many other times had his people forgotten the mighty works of Yahweh? So it is with us. We need to collect our share of memorial stones, remembering the times that God showed us his faithfulness, provision, and compassionate love, so that we don't fall into the trap of worrying about the future. One pastor went so far as to define sin as "forgetfulness." Surely, if we forget God's goodness, his grace and justice, his constant intervention in our lives, we will stray from his path.

One way to build a strong memory is by meditating on his ways. Meditation is to the mind as digestion is to the body; it is actually chewing, tasting, savoring, and finally, swallowing the morsels of truth. Psalm 1 compares the meditating man to a tree planted by streams of water, yielding fruit in its season, and prospering in whatever he does: "Blessed is the man who does not walk in the counsel of the wicked or stand in the way of sinners or sit in the seat of mockers. But his delight is in the law of the LORD, and on his law he meditates day and night. He is like a tree" (vv. 1–3).

But such a mental exercise isn't always easy, as J. I. Packer explains in his classic book *Knowing God:*

> Meditation is a lost art today and Christian people suffer grievously from their ignorance of the practice. Meditation is the activity of calling to mind, and thinking over, and dwelling on, and applying to oneself, the various things that one knows about the works and ways and purposes and promises of God. It is an activity of holy thought, consciously performed in the presence of God, under the eye of God, by the help of God; as a means of communion with God. Its purpose is to clear one's mental and spiritual vision of God, and to let His truth make its full and proper impact on one's mind and heart. It is a matter of talking to oneself about oneself; it is, indeed, often a matter of arguing with oneself, reasoning oneself out of moods of doubt and unbelief into a clear apprehension of God's power and grace. Its effect is ever to humble us, as we contemplate God's greatness and glory, and our own littleness and sinfulness, and to encourage and reassure us—"comfort" us, in the old, strong, Bible sense of the word—as we contemplate the unsearchable riches of divine mercy displayed in the Lord Jesus Christ. . . . As we enter more and more deeply into this experience of being humbled and exalted,

179

our knowledge of God increases, and with it our peace, our strength, and our joy.[7]

So as we meditate on God's power and grace, standing before the Lord (Gen. 18:22), seeking his face (1 Chron. 16:11), keeping his presence in our hearts (Luke 2:51), the light of God (Isa. 60:19) shines in even the most daunting darkness and we are not afraid. As David reminds us in his psalm of thanks in 1 Chronicles 16, the object of our contemplation and meditation is not an abstract idea but a person, someone for whom every human yearns. Someone who parts rivers and makes a path through what seems impossible.

A glance over one of my personal favorites, Psalm 119, also will remind us how our memory, meditation, and contemplation are related to our solid faith and balanced lifestyle. We are struck by all that the psalmist calls us to reflect on and cling to: God's statutes (divinely revealed teaching), precepts (detailed rules for life), commands (the express will of Israel's Lord), decrees (rulings written down), laws (verdicts of the divine Judge), and Word (communication of God's will to his people). Though much of this psalm reflects the tension and distress inherent in trying to live a righteous life in an unrighteous world, there is no question where the writer's strength comes from to persevere. He has not hidden himself away in some spiritual ivory tower, but he has chosen to remain in the hustle and strains of this world, pulled in many directions, yet anchored in the reality that, "Great peace have they who love your law, and *nothing* can make them stumble" (v. 165 emphasis mine).

An excellent way to meditate, then, is by finding what I call "perspective builders." These are the places that nurture our contemplative attitudes, soul-stirring locations that help us focus our thoughts and remind us who is in charge. For me, it's sitting beside the ocean or a mountain stream with paper, pen, Bible, and a book. For others, it's hiking in the woods or sitting in their favorite corner of a familiar diner or room considering the letters of Paul or writing a letter to God. "My thinkin' place," as one friend calls it.

Where's your "thinkin' place"? Why is it the location where you do your best thinking, where you come away with a renewed sense of perspective and insight?

Nature reflects the Almighty's creative ways and has a soothing way of refreshing our souls. A few years ago I took an incredible bicycling trip through Ireland's Dingle Peninsula. Along coastal cliffs and sheepy hills, I rode with friends through some of nature's most captivating "poems." The church and castle ruins were mystical, the pubs quaint, the sea air fresh and rich and full of wonder. Everywhere I looked—and smelled and listened—was a contemplative feast.

On day four of our trip we discovered a tiny island called Blasket, three miles across the bay, green and rugged and beautiful. It was here that some of Ireland's most poetic writing emerged from a group of farmers and fishermen. Exposed to the mighty mood swings of the ocean and the political powers of the land, the Islanders (as they came to be called) knew survival depended on being alert: Alert to the sounds of thunder, the looming clouds of dark rain, the salty wind that slapped its way into their daily existence. Every change in a day's weather from morning to night, from season to season, meant life for their small village of 150 or so rosy-faced folks.

No wonder they were a creative lot; they *had* to pay attention to the stuff of living. They had no formal education to rely on—they didn't learn to write until a few English poets visited and taught them as adults in the early 1900s. And they barely had an inkling about the world beyond theirs. To them, fishing, potatoes, and stories, mixed with a regular venture to Sunday church across the bay—weather permitting—were what mattered most.

I could see why. There, nature feeds creativity. The scenes themselves are always on the point of bursting into poetry. No doubt, the lush green hills and white sea breaking against jagged cliffs provided a steady diet of inspiration for the Islanders. The sea gave both daily sustenance and a healthy dose of terror and admiration, what one scholar called a "deep-seated belief in the kinship of man and nature, both subject to the same cycle of day and night, summer and winter, birth and death."[8]

And so they wrote. Not pithy captions of sentimental nature scenes, but words of art and substance and inexhaustible vitality. Like the others, Tomas O'Crohan, the island's best writer-fisherman-farmer, was determined to record life with "high literary merit coming out of an oral culture, triumphs of determination to master the written word, to leave a record of what life was like in my time and the neighbors that lived with me."[9] That life also included playing music from instruments they made themselves. And sculpting furniture from driftwood. And telling stories. And laughing. From the mid-1800s to the time the island was abandoned in 1953 (survival had met its match), these creative, (formally) uneducated artist-fishermen and women produced nearly twenty-five remarkable books written in Irish (Gaelic) and now translated into several languages. Why? Because a feast of life surrounded them and they partook. As one of their own writers observed, "I sat down on the bank above the beach where I had a splendid view around me. Dead indeed is the heart from which the balmy air of the sea cannot banish sorrow and grief."[10]

Obviously, we can learn much about life from traveling, whether it's through books and art or discussions and adventures with others. Whatever the form—from memorizing Scripture or singing hymns to sitting in a meadow or listening to a poem—the contemplative life can be found anywhere, taking us places we've never been before and making us into people we've always hoped to be, who live and breathe and have our being in the one who breathes life into us. Without active, contemplative minds, our faith will be bland and our lives will become stale.

And so, the call to contemplation is unmistakably a call each day to our Savior and Shepherd, the one who still says, "Come to me, all you who are weary and burdened, and I will give you rest. Take my yoke upon you and *learn* from me, for I am gentle and humble in heart, and you will find rest for your souls. For my yoke is easy and my burden is light" (Matt. 11:28–30 emphasis mine).

How does Matthew 11:28–30 relate to your life right now? Take a few contemplative moments to receive Christ's rest and care for your soul.

183

10

The Dessert Tray

Always do right. This will gratify some people and astonish the rest.

MARK TWAIN

When I was growing up in the foothills of the Colorado Rocky Mountains, I loved winter. As a young girl, winter meant putting on my brother's hand-me-down ice skates, lacing them up real tight, and venturing out onto a frozen lake or the local ice-skating rink. I'd bundle up in layers of sweaters and long underwear, walk real slow, and then plant myself on the slickness beneath me, hopeful for some small miracle that I'd actually stand up. I was not very good at this winter sport; I could barely slide an inch with the two skinny blades under my feet. Clumsy, awkward, and grabbing for any passing stability, I'd stumble a few feet, start to go down, recover my balance, and slide a few more feet only to go through the same motions all over again. It was a continual tug-of-war. Eventually, though, no amount of trying could compete with gravity's pull and down I'd go with a thunk, hitting the rock-hard, cold ice. I hated falling, not because I looked foolish—everyone looked silly with those uncomfortable skates on their feet. No, I hated falling for one simple reason: It hurt. Though I loved the cold air on my face, the Colorado blue sky above me, and the hot chocolate when it was over, ice-skating was never fun for me unless I was able to keep my balance.

The same is true for each of us as we encounter the sometimes cold, sometimes icy-hard moments we call life. Our good God and Creator certainly intended that we enjoy this earthly time, even in the midst of wintry challenges and awkward moments. He promised that his joy would be our strength (Neh. 8:10), his hope would be our healing (Prov. 13:12), and his praise would be our freedom (1 Peter 2:9). Ours is a heavenly Father who actively and personally participates in our "skating lessons," eager to see us glide through the days with grace and confidence, cheering us on and holding us up as we let him. Yes, he knows the ground is often slick and hard, that we're likely to go down every now and then, but it is he who keeps the universe in his palm and reminds us daily that nothing is too difficult for him. (After all, he once walked across a lake that *wasn't* frozen!) The good news of Christ is that *this* God has not left us alone.

Nor has he has left us to figure out life on our own. The principles and priorities that come with a balanced life are signposts for the journey, reminders to pay attention to them each day we venture out into the cold, or else suffer the consequences. By now we know that if we don't keep our spiritual equilibrium by spending solitary time with God, if we slide past the joy of serving others, if we avoid grabbing some-one else's arm for stability or community, and if we fail to focus or contemplate on each step we take, we fall. Thunk, down we go. And it hurts. Pain in itself is a good incentive for us to keep our balance and stay anchored in our faith.

But lest we think we're the only one who comes up scarred or bruised, we need also to look at those around us. The influence of our balanced Christian lifestyles extends far beyond our little ice-skating rinks. Indeed, our righteous lives (hidden in Christ) not only protect us from sin's slip-pery slope, but they bring the sweet aroma of Christ's Good News to a world that has lost its sense of purpose. When we fail to keep our spiritual balance in this spinning world, we run the risk of blending into the crowd rather than shin-ing like lights in front of it. Christians, of all people, should live such attractive, peaceful, and compassionate lives under the direction of their gracious Lord that others lit-erally come off the bench and ask if they can join us. Yes, when we stay active and balanced in our faith, when we partake of God's unmovable feast, the rewards—for every-one—are great. Spiritual desserts, I like to call them.

Make a list of all the things in your life for which you are thankful. How does such gratitude change your heart?

Perfect Peace

Throughout these pages, we've explored how integrating four essential ingredients into our lives ultimately produces

187

an energetic, balanced faith in the midst of busy schedules and daily demands. Just as we are supposed to include the four basic physical food groups into our daily diet to keep us healthy and strong, so, too, do we need regular helpings of these spiritual foods. We need solitude with God to restore, refresh, change, and direct us. Out of that time comes a natural outflow of justice-oriented and merciful service with others. Community, or challenging, supportive relationships with other believers, helps us reflect Christ's character and witness to the world. And the contemplation of truth in a variety of forms renews our minds so we will function effectively and honestly in this Christian life. Many counselors suggest that anger, fear, depression, or negative patterns are the result of faulty thinking, which, in turn, produces unhealthy relationships. Imagine what happens to the balanced Christian, then, who takes seriously the words of the prophet Isaiah, "You will keep in perfect peace him whose mind is steadfast [or stayed on thee]" (26:3).

But I want to be really clear: Though these four principles provide a helpful checklist for keeping "perfect peace" during times of stress or susceptibility, there are some things these four principles are *not*. When we daily focus our minds on the Triune nature of God, then every area of our life reflects his. It is God, through the person of Jesus Christ and the power of his Holy Spirit, who alone sustains us, corrects us, encourages us, and balances us—*not* four spiritual food groups. We must not view these principles as a magic formula for instant spiritual formation. For the Christian, there is no such thing as "instant maturity." Our love for God and reception of his love for us is an ongoing process that occurs in a multitude of ways—these four values simply provide helpful priorities to keep us enjoying the feast.

However, no two Christians are alike because God has made us all unique, imparting individual gifts, talents, and personalities to each of us. The working out of our salvation might look differently, for instance, to the rural Christian than it does the urban believer, just as the faith of a Brazilian Christian might look different from that of the African or North American. The apostle Paul said in Philippians 3:12, "Not that I have already obtained all this, or have already been made perfect, but I press on to take hold of that for which Christ Jesus took hold of me." Our commonality, then, is found in "that which Christ Jesus took hold of," and so we are never called to condemn or criticize one another but to encourage our fellow pilgrims on the road, wherever we may be. We are all "in process," being shaped and molded by the relentless grace of God. Maybe that's why Dietrich Bonhoeffer wrote in his book on community, *Life Together*, that "we are bound together by faith, not by experience. For Jesus Christ alone is our unity. Through him alone do we have access to one another, joy in one another, and fellowship with one another."[1]

We also must not allow these four values to become a substitute for the healthy embracing of mystery and uncertainty in life. Obviously, we cannot know all there is to know about living with Christ while we are restrained in these earthly human temples. He is God; we are not. Period. And that can be a difficult reality for Western believers who like to be in charge and organize and strategize every detail of every day. Yet, how many times have we thought our lives were going in one direction when suddenly some event (or divine intervention) changed the course entirely? Therefore, we are probably better off right now if we acknowledge truthfully that we are not in control of our lives and never will be. No, we were bought with a price (1 Cor. 7:23), and our lives are not our own. Thankfully, that means we do not have to have all the answers or the ability to plan every part of our lives for the next fifty years. God is able, and "the mystery of godliness is great" (1 Tim. 3:16). Our part simply is to yield to his mysterious ways and press into his presence.

Finally, we must remember that these four food groups are not their counterfeits. Solitude is not an easy escape from the stress of relationships; service is not a feel-good patronizing act of charity; community is not unlimited permission to impose on other people, creating unhealthy, draining dependencies; and contemplation is not a purposeless, intellectual exercise or avoidance of emotions. When authentic, these food groups can never operate independent of each other if active balance is to be attained. When authentic, they are interdependent and always for the good of God's kingdom.

Paul perfectly described these tensions in Colossians 2:2–5:

> My purpose is that they may be encouraged in heart and united in love [true community], so that they may have the full riches of complete understanding, in order that they may know the mystery of God [true contemplation], namely, Christ, in whom are hidden all the treasures of wisdom and knowledge [true solitude]. I tell you this [true service] so that no one may deceive you by fine-sounding arguments. For though I am absent from you in body, I am present with you in spirit and delight to see how orderly [balanced] you are and how firm your faith in Christ is.

Scan in your mind
the contents of your life.
Have the counterfeit spiritual food
groups crept in at all?
Ask God to keep you pure and blameless
and to keep your mind in perfect peace.

Sweet Benefits

One of my favorite questions in life is, "So what?" Please understand that I mean no disrespect when I ask it. It is not a callous response to information but rather an honest attempt to bring it home in practical terms, to help me in the now. So, I ask, what good will it do to try to live a balanced Christian life? In other words, we know what happens when we don't live a balanced radical life for Christ. What happens when we do? What are the rewards, the benefits, the desserts, if you will?

A benefit is a noun, a thing one has or receives. It is an "advantage; profit, an act of kindness." When something is beneficial, it is helpful, profitable, charitable. Likewise, a reward is a "repayment or prize for merit or accomplishment, profit, recompense, gain." We already know how an active relationship with Christ brings us protection, shielding us from the hurt and pain of falling, even preventing the possible injuries—to ourselves and those around us—that come from losing our footing. Balance has its advantages; everyone profits or gains something when our lives reflect the Master of the universe. In fact, there are a variety of sweet benefits and rewards that a balanced spiritual diet brings.

Proverbs 3:1–2 reminds us, for instance, that in keeping God's commands in our hearts, we will enjoy long life and prosperity. A chapter later in verses 21 and 22, we are encouraged not to "let them out of your sight, keep them within your heart; for they are life to those who find them and health to a man's whole body." Timothy tells us in 1 Timothy 6:17–19 that in being rich in good deeds, and putting our hope in God "who richly provides us with everything for our enjoyment . . . [we] take hold of the life that is truly life." This good life, this prosperous life is not to be confused with the American ideal for wealth and comfort.

In contrast, life with Christ brings us riches and health this world knows little of. Simple things like walking through parks in the autumn, listening to a child sing, smelling a rose, telling a stranger about Christ's love, or sharing spaghetti dinners with close friends become treasures that are worth far more than jewels or diamonds. Indeed, they help us experience the abundant life (John 10:10) Jesus promises us in himself.

And that's not all. Balance brings much-needed rest to our souls (Matt. 11:28; Heb. 4:9–11), peace (Prov. 14:30; Col. 3:15), grace (Rom. 5:17), compassion (Lam. 3:22–23), and hope, which is "an anchor for the soul, firm and secure" (Heb. 6:19). These gifts keep us from turning to the left or the right, guarding our hearts along the way, and infusing us with the necessary strength to "press on toward the goal to win the prize for which God has called me heavenward in Christ Jesus" (Phil. 3:14). We are blessed with "every spiritual blessing in Christ" (Eph. 1:3) and, consequently, experience an inexpressible joy (2 Cor. 8:2) that overflows onto others. There's little doubt that a balanced, abundant, grace-filled radical life with Jesus can do anything but affect others with the same!

We also experience direction, purpose, and impact as we walk in relationship with God (2 Cor. 5:17–21) as well as the ongoing sustenance of God's love when we partake of his feast (Ps. 23:5–6; Rev. 7:16). Our souls are encouraged, which in turn, encourage others (Heb. 12:1–5), our attitudes are changed as are others (Eph. 4:23), and we are formed more and more into the image of his likeness (Rom. 8:29), thereby challenging others to do the same. Yes, true Christianity is a wonderfully contagious thing! And so our unbelieving friends and family who—like us—long for order and peace in what seems like a chaotic world can't help but see the light of hope in us. We know the one who set the earth in place, the Prince of Peace, and when we walk a balanced, full life with him, he is lifted up for their sake. It's a win-win situation. As Henri J. Nouwen said, "The compassionate life is a grateful life, and actions born out of gratefulness are not compulsive but free, not somber but joyful, not fanatical but liberating."[2]

Spend a few minutes reading and reflecting on the rewarding verses listed above.

Boundless Gifts

Inherent in the benefits and joys of a balanced Christian life are a healthy sense of limits, purpose, and vision. In order for us to stay focused on Christ, we have to be able to say no to some things and yes to others. We have to establish clear boundaries—those guidelines that serve to indicate the limits of anything, the limit itself. We would have many accidents on the roads if clear boundary lines were not painted in white and yellow for the cars, bicycles, and trucks that travel them. In the same way, we must be able to recognize our limits, protect our time, and exercise wisdom over our choices and schedules.

Boundaries are established when we know who God is (that we're not him) as well as when we know who we are, and who we aren't. For instance, we should likely say no to teaching the third grade Sunday school class at our local church once we've discovered our individual gifts lie not in creative communication but in, say, accounting. Then we could say yes to tutoring a neighbor child in math after school instead, or offering financial counseling to young

193

adults. We don't need to earn anyone's approval or feel guilty for saying no because our security and identity have already been established in Christ, who has revealed to us his purpose for our lives as well as the boundaries that protect it.

Assessing our purpose, gifts, and desires, then, can become an important step on the road to balance. I think one of the number one reasons people get burned out in the Christian life is because they don't know what they are uniquely born for. They spin their wheels trying everything, except that unique area God has gifted them for. First Peter 4:10 says, "Each one should use whatever gift he has received to serve others, faithfully administering God's grace in its various forms." When we don't discover our godly desires and talents (and they always go together) or utilize our gifts for God's grace, we disregard our purpose and everyone misses out. I have a friend who's extremely gifted at facilitating small group discussions around biblical themes. Yet, because she doesn't have either a college degree or a flexible schedule, she dismisses her gift as "unimportant" and so hasn't led a discussion in years. Meanwhile, she's constantly struggling to discover "what to do with my life" while the body of Christ is deprived of her God-given talents.

Spending time and energy on the right things is a crucial element for balance and for building God's kingdom. There's nothing more frustrating than not knowing what we're supposed to do, than walking aimlessly down the Christian path. No, most of us really want to be about our Father's business because we love him and desire to please him. A sense of boundaries, then, as well as an awareness of our unique gifts actually helps nurture our solitude, service, community, and contemplation. But these four food groups also help us set our boundaries and use our gifts as well. They are interdependent. I think William Barclay summed it up well in *The Beatitudes and the Lord's Prayer for Everyman:*

The way to power lies through the realization of helplessness; that the way to victory lies through the admission of defeat; that the way to goodness lies through the confession and the acknowledgment of sin. Herein is an essential truth which runs through all life. If a man is ill, the first necessity is that he should admit and recognize that he is ill, and that then he should seek for a cure in the right place. The way to knowledge begins with the admission of ignorance. The one man who can never learn is the man who thinks that he knows everything already. . . . The way to independence lies through dependence, and the way to freedom lies through surrender. If ever a man is to be independent of the chances and the changes of life, that independence must come from his complete dependence on God. If ever a man is to know true freedom, that freedom must come through complete surrender to God. . . . The way to bliss which the world can neither give nor take away lies through the recognition of our own need and the conviction that the need can be met, when we commit to God in perfect trust.[3]

Acknowledge your trust in God right now by assessing your gifts, boundaries, and purpose.

Bon Appétit!

Developing an integrity of faith, that is, a healthy vibrant witness that reflects the Triune God, is the ultimate privilege and joy for the Christian. It comes when we are in his presence, when we reach out to others in compassionate, mutual care, when we build up his body, and when we con-

195

sider the glorious wonders of his love and kingdom. These four spiritual food groups lead us into a closer walk with the one who is always inviting us to a feast that is both unmovable and delicious, an eternal banquet that begins today. When we accept the invitation, we come to a table so glorious and exhilarating that we will be forever changed, a place where the head of the table looks into our eyes, smiles, and reminds us that "no eye has seen, no ear has heard, no mind has conceived what God has prepared for those who love him" (1 Cor. 2:9).

NOTES

Chapter 1: "Pass Me the Balance"

1. Malcolm Muggeridge, *Jesus Rediscovered* (New York: Doubleday, 1969), 48, quoted in *Conversions: The Christian Experience*, ed. Hugh T. Kerr and John M. Mulder (Grand Rapids: Eerdmans, 1983), 251.

2. Dietrich Bonhoeffer, *Life Together* (New York: Harper & Row, 1954).

Chapter 2: Solitude: Breakfast with Jesus

1. C. S. Lewis, *Surprised by Joy* (New York: Harcourt, Brace, and Co., 1955), 211–24, quoted in Kerr and Mulder, *Conversions*, 201–2.

2. Henri J. Nouwen, quoted in Dorothy Frick, "Time with God," *Virtue* (March–April 1966), 33.

3. Sister Wendy Beckett, *Meditations on Silence* (New York: Dorling Kindersley, 1995), 28.

4. John White, *The Fight* (Downers Grove, Ill.: InterVarsity Press, 1976).

Chapter 3: Solitude: Setting the Table for One

1. Henri J. Nouwen, *Out of Solitude* (Notre Dame: Ave Maria Press, 1974), quoted in Bob Benson Sr. and Michael W. Benson, *Disciplines for the Inner Life* (Nashville: Thomas Nelson, 1989), 199.

2. Catherine Calvert, "A Day of Solitude," *Victoria Magazine* (September 1997), 82.

3. Sara Park McLaughlin, *Meeting God in Silence: How a Time-Honored Spiritual Discipline Can Bring Meaning to Your Life* (Wheaton: Tyndale, 1993), 111.

4. Lewis, *Surprised by Joy*, quoted in Kerr and Mulder, *Conversions*, 200.

5. Mother Teresa, quoted in McLaughlin, *Meeting God in Silence*, 39.

Chapter 4: Service: Chopping Those Onions

1. Charles Dickens, *A Christmas Carol*, in *The Book of Virtues*, ed. William Bennett (New York: Simon and Schuster, 1993), 154.

2. Henri J. Nouwen, *Compassion: A Reflection on the Christian Life* (New York: Image/Doubleday, 1966), 17.

Chapter 5: Service: Working in the Kitchen

1. Martin Luther King Jr., "The Drum Major Instinct," in *A Testament of Hope: The Essential Writings of Martin Luther King Jr.*, ed. James Melvin Washington (San Francisco: Harper & Row, 1986), 265.

2. Nouwen, *Compassion*, 18.

3. Dorothy Day, *Little by Little*, in *Dorothy Day: Selected Writings*, ed. Robert Ellsberg (New York: Orbis Books, 1983), 87.

4. Waldron Scott, *Bring Forth Justice* (Grand Rapids: Eerdmans, 1980), 152, xvi.

5. Timothy J. Keller, *Ministries of Mercy: The Call of the Jericho Road* (Grand Rapids: Zondervan, 1989).

Chapter 6: Community: Sharing the Meal

1. Leo Tolstoy, *Where Love Is, There God Is Also*, ed. Lawrence Jordan (Nashville: Thomas Nelson, 1993), 35–48.

2. Koinonia House Interactive ONLINE, "Essays on the Trinity."

3. Nouwen, *Compassion*, 64.

4. Pastor Jeff White, "Community," Redeemer Presbyterian Church handout.

5. Elizabeth O'Connor, *Call to Commitment* (New York: Harper & Row, 1963).

Chapter 7: Community: Eating Together

1. Quoted in Benson and Benson, *Disciplines*, 137.

2. Julie Gorman, *Community That Is Christian*, quoted in White, "Community."

3. Bonhoeffer, *Life Together*.

4. Walter Wangerin Jr., *The Book of the Dun Cow* (New York: Harper & Row, 1978), 89.

Chapter 8: Contemplation: Savoring Each Morsel

1. Thomas Merton, *What Is Contemplation?* (Springfield, Ill.: Templegate Publishers, 1978).

2. Luci Shaw, "Transforming Life into Art," lecture, Festival of Faith and Writing Conference, Calvin College, Grand Rapids, Michigan, 1996.

3. Richard J. Foster, *Celebration of Discipline: The Path to Spiritual Growth* (San Francisco: Harper & Row, 1988), 54.

Chapter 9: Contemplation: Taste, Smell, Enjoy

1. Ray Bradbury, *Fahrenheit 451* (New York: Ballantine Books, 1953), 74.

2. John Murray, "The Solace of Words: Literature and Suffering," *The Bloomsbury Review* 12, no. 5 (July–August 1992), 21.

3. Leland Ryken, *Realms of God: The Classics in Christian Perspective* (Wheaton: Harold Shaw, 1991), 110.

4. Walter Wangerin Jr., "What's a Good Story?" *The Lutheran*, 11 July 1990, 5.

5. Flannery O'Connor, *Mystery and Manners*, ed. Sally and Robert Fitzgerald (New York: Farrar, Straus, and Giroux, 1957), 167.

6. Quoted in Harold Fickett, *Flannery O'Connor: Images of Grace* (Grand Rapids: Eerdmans, 1986), 38.

7. J. I. Packer, *Knowing God*, quoted in Benson and Benson, *Disciplines*, 109.

8. From a museum brochure at the Blasket Island Museum Centre.

9. From a museum plaque at the Blasket Island Museum Centre.

10. Ibid.

Chapter 10: The Dessert Tray

1. Bonhoeffer, *Life Together*, 39.

2. Nouwen, *Compassion*, 126.

3. William Barclay, *The Beatitudes and the Lord's Prayer for Everyman*, quoted in Benson and Benson, *Disciplines*, 281.

BIBLIOGRAPHY

Angelou, Maya. *I Know Why the Caged Bird Sings*. New York: Random House, 1969.

Arnold, Christoph. *Why We Live in Community: The Bruderhof*. Farmington, Pa.: Plough Press, 1995.

Augustine. *Confessions*. Commentary by James J. O'Donnell. Oxford: Oxford University Press, 1992.

Bakke, Ray. *The Urban Christian*. Madison: Two Thousand One Hundred Productions, 1987.

Beckett, Sister Wendy. *Meditations on Silence*. New York: Dorling Kindersley, 1995.

Benson, Bob, Sr., and Michael W. Benson, *Disciplines for the Inner Life*. Nashville: Thomas Nelson, 1989.

Bloom, Allan. *The Closing of the American Mind*. New York: Touchstone Books, 1987.

Bonhoeffer, Dietrich. *Life Together*. New York: Harper & Row, 1954.

Bradbury, Ray. *Fahrenheit 451*. New York: Ballantine Books, 1953.

Calvert, Catherine. "A Day of Solitude." *Victoria Magazine* (September 1997).

Cavanagh, Michael. "Cognitive Development: Pastoral Implications." Quoted in *Current Thoughts and Trends* (May 1996).

Chesterton, G. K. *The Man Who Was Thursday: A Nightmare*. New York: Boni and Liveright, 1908.

Coles, Robert. *The Call of Stories: Teaching and Moral Imagination*. Boston: Houghton Mifflin, 1989.

Colson, Charles W. *Loving God*. Grand Rapids: Zondervan, 1983.

Dawn, Marva J. *The Hilarity of Community: Romans 12 and How to Be the Church*. Grand Rapids: Eerdmans, 1992.

Day, Dorothy. *Little by Little*. In *Dorothy Day: Selected Writings*, edited by Robert Ellsberg. New York: Orbis Books, 1983.

Dickens, Charles. *A Christmas Carol*. In *The Book of Virtues*, edited by William Bennett. New York: Simon and Schuster, 1993.

Dillard, Annie. *The Writing Life*. New York: HarperPerennial, 1989.

Dostoyevsky, Fyodor. *The Brothers Karamazov*. Translated by Constance Garnett. Revised and edited by Ralph E. Matlaw. New York: Norton, 1976.

Fickett, Harold. *Flannery O'Connor: Images of Grace*. Grand Rapids: Eerdmans, 1986.

Finney, Jack. *Invasion of the Body Snatchers*. New York: Simon and Schuster, 1954.

Foster, Richard J. *Celebration of Discipline: The Path to Spiritual Growth*. San Francisco: Harper & Row, 1988.

————. *Freedom of Simplicity*. New York: HarperPaperbacks, 1981.

Gardner, John W. *Excellence: Can We Be Equal and Excellent Too?* New York: Norton, 1984.

Gates, Henry Louis, and Nellie Y. McKay, eds. *The Norton Anthology of African American Literature*. New York: Norton, 1996.

Greene, Graham. *The Potting Shed: A Play in Three Acts*. London: Heinemann, 1958.

Hawthorne, Nathaniel. *The Scarlet Letter*. New York: Dodd, Mead, 1948.

Jordan-Lake, Joy. *Grit and Grace: Portraits of a Woman's Life*. Wheaton: Harold Shaw, 1997.

Kadlecek, Jo, and Pamela Toussaint. *I Call You Friend: Four Women's Stories of Race, Faith, and Friendship*. Nashville: Broadman and Holman, 1999.

Keller, Timothy J. *Ministries of Mercy: The Call of the Jericho Road*. Grand Rapids: Zondervan, 1989.

Kerr, Hugh T., and John M. Mulder, eds. *Conversions: The Christian Experience*. Grand Rapids: Eerdmans, 1983.

Koinonia House Interactive ONLINE, Inc., P.O. Box D, Coeur d'Alene, ID 83816. http://www.khouse.org/study.html, "Essays on the Trinity."

Lawrence, Brother. *The Practice of the Presence of God*. Uhrichsville, Ohio: Barbour and Company, 1993.

L'Engle, Madeleine. *Walking on Water: Reflections on Faith and Art*. Wheaton: Harold Shaw, 1980.

Lewis, C. S. *Mere Christianity*. New York: Touchstone, 1980.

Loewen, James. *Lies My Teacher Told Me: Everything Your American History Textbook Got Wrong*. New York: Touchstone Books, 1995.

Lupton, Robert. *Theirs Is the Kingdom: Celebrating the Gospel in Urban America*. San Francisco: HarperSanFrancisco, 1989.

McLaughlin, Sara Park. *Meeting God in Silence: How a Time-Honored Spiritual Discipline Can Bring Meaning to Your Life*. Wheaton: Tyndale, 1993.

Merton, Thomas. *What Is Contemplation?* Springfield, Ill.: Templegate Publishers, 1978.

Monroe, Kelly, ed. *Finding God at Harvard.* Grand Rapids: Zondervan, 1996.

Muggeridge, Malcolm. *A Third Testament.* Boston: Little, Brown, 1976.

Murray, John. "The Solace of Words: Literature and Suffering." *The Bloomsbury Review* 12, no. 5 (1992).

Nouwen, Henri J., Donald P. McNeill, and Douglas A. Morrison. *Compassion: A Reflection on the Christian Life.* Garden City, N.Y.: Doubleday, 1982.

O'Connor, Flannery. *Everything That Rises Must Converge.* New York: Farrar, Straus, and Giroux, 1965.

———. *A Good Man Is Hard to Find.* New York: Harcourt, Brace, 1955.

———. *The Habit of Being.* Edited by Sally Fitzgerald. New York: Vintage Books, 1979.

———. *Mystery and Manners.* Edited by Sally and Robert Fitzgerald. New York: Farrar, Straus, and Giroux, 1957.

Perkins, John, with Jo Kadlecek. *Resurrecting Hope: Powerful Stories of How God Is Moving to Reach the Cities.* Ventura, Calif.: Regal, 1995.

Peterson, Eugene. *A Long Obedience in the Same Direction: Discipleship in an Instant Society.* Downers Grove, Ill.: InterVarsity Press, 1980.

Potok, Chaim. *My Name Is Asher Lev.* New York: Fawcett Columbine, 1972.

Raybon, Patricia. *My First White Friend.* New York: Viking Penguin, 1997.

Ryken, Leland. *The Liberated Imagination: Thinking Christianly about the Arts.* Wheaton: Harold Shaw, 1989.

———. *Realms of God: The Classics in Christian Perspective.* Wheaton: Harold Shaw, 1991.

Scott, Waldron. *Bring Forth Justice: A Contemporary Perspective on Mission.* Grand Rapids: Eerdmans, 1980.

Shaw, Luci. *Polishing the Petoskey Stone: New and Selected Poems.* Wheaton: Harold Shaw, 1990.

Sherman, Amy L. *Restorers of Hope: Reaching the Poor in Your Community with Church-Based Ministries That Work.* Wheaton: Crossway Books, 1997.

Shuler, Clarence. *Winning the Race to Unity: Is Racial Reconciliation Really Working?* Chicago: Moody, 1998.

Stott, John. *Balanced Christianity.* Downers Grove, Ill.: InterVarsity Press, 1975.

Thurman, Howard. *Jesus and the Disinherited.* Boston: Beacon Press, 1976.

Tolstoy, Leo. *Where Love Is, There God Is Also.* Edited by Lawrence Jordan. Nashville: Thomas Nelson, 1993.

Veith, Gene Edward. *The Gift of Art: The Place of the Arts in Scripture.* Downers Grove, Ill.: InterVarsity Press, 1983.

———. *Reading between the Lines: A Christian Approach to Literature.* Wheaton: Crossway Books, 1990.

Wallis, Jim. *The Call to Conversion*. San Francisco: HarperSanFrancisco, 1982.

Wangerin, Walter, Jr. *The Book of the Dun Cow*. New York: Harper & Row, 1978.

———. *Miss Lil and the Chronicles of Grace*. San Francisco: Harper & Row, 1988.

———. *Ragman and Other Cries of Faith*. San Francisco: Harper & Row, 1984.

———. "What's a Good Story?" *The Lutheran*, 11 July 1990, 5.

Washington, James Melvin, ed. *A Testament of Hope: The Essential Writings of Martin Luther King Jr.* San Francisco: Harper & Row, 1986.

Yancey, Philip, ed. *Reality and the Vision: Eighteen Contemporary Writers Tell Who They Read and Why*. Dallas: Word, 1990.

———. *What's So Amazing about Grace?* Grand Rapids: Zondervan, 1997.

Jo Kadlecek is a freelance writer and journalist who has lived out her commitment to being a neighbor by living and working in urban contexts for the last decade. With master of arts degrees from both Regent University and the University of Colorado at Denver, she has taught communications and English courses to adult, college, and high school students on several Christian and secular campuses. She has coauthored a number of books, including *Resurrecting Hope: Powerful Stories of How God Is Reaching the Cities* (Regal) and *I Call You Friend: Four Women's Stories of Race, Faith, and Friendship* (Broadman and Holman), and her writing has been featured in *The Saturday Evening Post*, *Christianity Today*, and *Discipleship Journal*. She resides with her husband, a pastor, in New York City.